T0329520

Grading Health Care

Pamela P. Hanes
Merwyn R. Greenlick
Editors

Foreword by Edward B. Perrin

Grading
Health Care

The Science and Art of Developing
Consumer Scorecards

Jossey-Bass Publishers • San Francisco

Copyright © 1998 by Jossey-Bass Inc., Publishers, 350 Sansome Street, San Francisco, California 94104.

All rights reserved. No part of this publication may be reproduced, stored in a retrieval system, or transmitted, in any form or by any means, electronic, mechanical, photocopying, recording, or otherwise, without the prior written permission of the publisher.

Jossey-Bass books and products are available through most bookstores. To contact Jossey-Bass directly, call (888) 378-2537, fax to (800) 605-2665, or visit our website at www.josseybass.com.

Substantial discounts on bulk quantities of Jossey-Bass books are available to corporations, professional associations, and other organizations. For details and discount information, contact the special sales department at Jossey-Bass.

For sales outside the United States, please contact your local Simon & Schuster International Office.

Library of Congress Cataloguing-in-Publication Data

Grading health care : the science and art of developing consumer
    scorecards / Pamela P. Hanes and Merwyn R. Greenlick, editors.
        p. cm.
    Includes index.
    ISBN 0-7879-4027-5
    1. Medical care—United States—Quality control. 2. Managed
care plans (Medical care)—United States. 3. Consumer education—
United States. I. Hanes, Pamela. II. Greenlick, Merwyn R.
RA399.A3G73 1998
362.1'068'5—dc21   98-4892
                                                                              CIP

FIRST EDITION
HB Printing   10 9 8 7 6 5 4 3 2 1

Contents

Foreword

It is a pleasure to introduce this truly innovative and timely volume on the art and science of developing consumer scorecards. We are currently witnessing a phenomenal growth of scholarly and market-initiated activity related to the development of consumer information materials and health plan scorecards. This activity has been encouraged by an environment in which health care goods and services are rapidly being transformed into market commodities.

Consumer information projects are proliferating at all levels of the health care system from individual health plans to regional, state, and federal efforts. Included is the federal sponsorship of the Consumer Assessment of Health Plan Survey (CAHPS), a five-year initiative being sponsored by the U.S. Department of Health and Human Services Agency for Health Care Policy and Research. The recent endorsement by President Clinton of a Consumer's Bill of Rights in Health Care is yet another manifestation of the growing importance of this dynamic area of health policy.

Underpinning all these efforts is the belief that for a health care market to perform optimally, informed and value-conscious consumers are required. In spite of economic theory holding that markets are optimized by symmetrical relationships between producers and (individual) consumers, most existing efforts at quantifying, measuring, and reporting quality and value in health care have been focused on the information needs of volume purchasers such as large employer groups and the federal and state governments.

I was fortunate to have participated in the Oregon Consumer Scorecard Project in an advisory capacity. It was clear from the outset that Drs. Hanes and Greenlick and the project staff were breaking new ground as they set out to better understand the information needs of consumers and how those needs could be translated into useable information for decision-making purposes. The literature was lean and the need for enlightenment great.

The unique contribution of the Oregon Consumer Scorecard Consortium effort is its focus on the information needs of the system's heaviest users—individuals with significant chronic health conditions and disabilities. The strength of the material presented in this volume is its ability to relate in understandable and engaging ways how the marriage of art and science is possible in scorecard development, even in the present volatile and politically charged environment. The authors provide concrete examples of the many challenges and opportunities they faced in their work, taking the reader through the background thinking and experimentation, and the lessons learned from all aspects of scorecard development.

Grading Health Care offers lessons to be applied and tips to be used for a broad range of audiences. Health plan managers will be interested in this book because of the numerous examples of theory-to-practice that can inform their internal quality improvement efforts. The book is a good introduction to the underlying science of developing consumer satisfaction surveys and quality performance monitoring activities. State policymakers will benefit from the discussions of managing multiple and varied stakeholder interests in pursuit of the common goal of quality improvement in health care. The book is filled with helpful hints about managing the disparate interests of key stakeholders ranging from state bureaucrats to health plans to consumer groups.

We can anticipate that for at least the next several years, consumer information projects will continue to flourish as we test market principles in the delivery of health care. The promise and the limitations of the scorecard methodology are honestly discussed in this volume. Most policy analysts and health care providers agree on one issue: quality standards in health care must not be sacrificed for the sake of efficiency and cost containment. A major question, if not the major issue in this trade-off, is how well a market-driven health care system is serving the needs of its customers. To be attentive to those needs requires new consumer-oriented measurement tools and reporting mechanisms. *Grading Health Care* makes an important contribution to moving this agenda forward.

Seattle, Washington   EDWARD B. PERRIN
March 1998

To our extraordinary progeny: David, Timothy, and Rachel Hanes, Michael and Vicki Greenlick, and Phyllis Greenlick Tabor

Preface

This book can be viewed as an intellectual journey through uncharted policymaking territory. We, as members of the Oregon Consumer Scorecard Consortium, considered whether it is possible for government to make policy that will benefit consumers of health care. Specifically, we explored the question of whether scorecards can be constructed to help guide consumers in their efforts to choose a health plan, even as the health care landscape in Oregon—and throughout the nation—becomes more and more unrecognizable.

Although health care systems are changing throughout the world, the health care delivery system in Oregon has been particularly affected by the forces of change, leaving providers, consumers, and those responsible for policy formulation simultaneously concerned, worried, and hopeful.

As the Oregon Consumer Scorecard Consortium began its journey, the intellectual perspective we embraced was derived from a period often described as the golden age of American medicine: the fee-for-service, private-practice medical care system of the mid-twentieth century. Experiences from the journey have shifted our thinking toward a systems view that is more consistent with the population-based, capitated health care organizations we will all be dealing with in the twenty-first century.

Some among the traveling party were concerned that we had embarked on a fool's mission. The path to a model consumer scorecard that is designed to help consumers make informed choices among health plans was not guided by a road map already in existence. Certainly, we were daunted by the intellectual and practical obstacles we encountered. Although others before us had headed in the same direction, most had returned without reaching their goal.

What we present in this book is a road map, albeit a primitive one, that shows one way to reach the destination we sought: the production of a useful choice and purchasing tool for consumers. The volume also presents a traveler's guide to some of the more interesting scenic attractions along the way. We offer guidance and support for those who choose to undertake the challenge, whether they are naive or well-seasoned travelers.

Most of us in the consortium have come to believe that ours was not a fool's journey. Having now arrived at a stopping place, we think we have produced a thing of real value. We also acknowledge that the idealized consumer-oriented scorecard described throughout this volume has yet to be developed.

However, there is a valid basis for the fears and skepticism that plague many travelers on the scorecard path. There is no clear, direct way to proceed. The practical, hands-on information provided in this volume will be useful to those interested in creating a health plan scorecard for consumers, and it can provide a great deal of technical and common-sense guidance. But it does not contain the full complement of technological tools necessary to develop a model consumer scorecard. Such a tool box does not exist. A consumer scorecard that is tailored to the individualized information needs of consumers will probably not be available for a good many years. We do think it is possible to produce a scorecard that can help consumers in the decision-making process. That is a bold statement—one we could not have made with any degree of assurance when we began the journey described in this book.

The impetus for developing health plan scorecards came from large purchasers, especially employers, whose motives are unclear. Many health care professionals suspect that employers would like to steer their employees to less expensive, rather than higher quality, health care services. However, these same major purchasers believe that specifying the dimensions of quality on which health plans are evaluated will change plans in positive ways, thus increasing the value of the services provided. They further believe that industry norms can be changed or modified with regard to the performance measures included on scorecards.

However, many of us become skilled at directing our learning so that we can pass examinations. Health plan administrators can probably do so as well. The Health Plan Employer Data Information System (HEDIS), which is discussed in chapters throughout this volume, certainly appears to have had this effect. For example, when health plan administrators were informed that their plan would be evaluated on the extent to which the recommended immunization series for two-year-olds was being completed for members, most set out to achieve this objective. By the time the next round of HEDIS measures are released, many, if not most, health plans will probably be reporting two-year-old immunization rates nearing 90 percent. The average health plan had a rate of around 50 percent (an optimistic calculation) at the beginning of the HEDIS process.

There was no such optimism among the consumers we talked with early in our project. In fact, most consumers were skeptical that scorecards could produce useful information for selecting from available health care options. These consumers were particularly skeptical about the health plan performance measures known as HEDIS measures because many did not seem relevant. As one woman in an Oregon focus group reportedly stated, "I don't care at all what proportion of a plan's population had a mammogram. What matters to me is if I can get a mammogram how and when I want one."

As you read this book, you will discover related issues, including the dimensions of health care delivery that are most important to consumers, and you will get a sense of how consumers would like to see a scorecard formatted. You will glimpse the struggles and challenges created by our current methodological limitations and have a peek at the political skirmishes inherent in the creation of a consumer scorecard. Although you should come to appreciate how these problems could vex those who undertake the journey, you will also receive some guidance on making the compromises necessary to achieve progress. And most important, you will come to understand that the choices you make will have consequences.

This book will help you understand that the journey reported here was made by people in a uniquely constituted group, with representatives from most of the possible interests contained in the field of health policy: consumers, researchers, policymakers, health professionals, and health-insuring organizations. This consortium model gave us the advantage of having a particularly broad perspective as we looked out over the road ahead. It also meant that we had the difficult task of satisfying a large, vocal, and at times unwieldy group. We hope that you will gain insight into the viewpoints, needs, desires, and contributions of this large cast of characters. Much of the richness of our story is reflected in this diversity.

Finally, we are pleased to assure the reader that those on the scorecard journey paid particular attention to two special populations of consumers who are frequently overlooked. First, for a variety of reasons, we focused on consumers who live in rural areas and therefore have limited options in arranging their health care. Second, we focused on individuals who have special health care needs such as serious chronic illness or disabling conditions. These populations are easily overlooked in scorecard development because their numbers are small; yet their information needs are great. The one universal theme expressed by consumers in Oregon, as elsewhere, is that choice information needs to be tailored to "people like me."

We very much enjoyed teaming up with our fellow travelers on this exciting but difficult journey. Our greatest rewards came from the interactions and experiences shared with our traveling companions and with those we met along the way. In that spirit, we offer this work to you.

Portland, Oregon   PAMELA P. HANES
March 1998   MERWYN R. GREENLICK

Acknowledgments

Many individuals made substantive contributions to the Oregon Consumer Scorecard Project. We would be remiss not to acknowledge the many and important contributions of our fellow travelers, particularly the Oregon Consumer Scorecard Consortium members. First and foremost, our thanks go to Vickie Gates, the former Oregon Health Plan Administrator, who had the vision and political acumen to suggest a consortium model as the appropriate vehicle for consumer scorecard development. She provided expert leadership, a quick wit, and lots of road stories along the way. To our friends and colleagues at the Agency for Health Care Policy and Research (AHCPR), Clifton Gaus, former director, and Sandra Robinson, our project officer, we owe a debt of gratitude for having the confidence and belief in the Oregon Consumer Scorecard Consortium to provide needed financial assistance for its journey. To our colleagues at the University of Washington's Rural Health Services Research Center, Ed Perrin and Sue Skillman, we owe much for their sharing of rural health research resources with Oregon to pursue this project. To each of our contributing authors in this volume, their respective accountings of the road trip typify the diversity of our traveling party. Finally, to each member of the consortium who gave countless hours and boundless energy to the endeavor, a hearty thank you.

Members of the *steering committee* were Bruce Bayley, Providence Health Systems; Bruce Bishop, Kaiser Permanente; Ralph Crawshaw, Oregon Health Decisions; Jeff Davis, Marion County

Health Department; Vickie Gates, Oregon Health Plan; Jeannette Hamby, Oregon state senate; David Lansky, Foundation for Accountability; David Lindquist, Oregon Medical Association; Lew Parker, Parker Printing; Ken Rutledge, Oregon Association of Hospitals and Health Systems; Dick Shoemaker, Office of Medical Assistance Programs; Barney Speight, The Benchmark Group; and Mylia Wray, Benova, Inc.

Members of the *health plan committee* were Julia Bartschi, Intercommunity Health Network; Diane Bennett, Benova, Inc.; Kathleen Cary, PacificCare of Oregon; Beverly Day, Evergreen Medical Systems & Family Care; Leslie Ellertson, PacificCare of Oregon; Dee Dee Frye, Oregon Dental Service Health Plan; Jim Gersback, Kaiser Permanente; Susan Gillett, SelectCare; Bruce Goldberg, Oregon Health Sciences University; Ted Harris, Good Health Plan of Oregon; Marlene Haugland, Office of Medical Assistance Programs; Patricia Korjenek, Blue Cross/Blue Shield of Oregon; Diane McMillian, PACC Health Plans; Jim Reyes, QualMed Health Plan; Carole Romm, CareOregon; Sharon Saty, Tuality Health Alliance; Barney Speight, The Benchmark Group; Roylene Waldron, Grants Pass Clinic Primary Care Organization; and Jaqi Wyatt, Medford Clinic.

Members of the *technical committee* were Berhanu Anteneh, Office of Medical Assistance Programs; Diane Bennett, Benova, Inc.; Jonathan Brown, Kaiser Permanente Center for Health Research; Julia Bryan-Wilson, Oregon Health Policy Institute; Ted Colombo, Kaiser Permanente (retired); Tina Edlund, Office of Medical Assistance Programs; Dan Harris, Health Resources Commission; Dawn Hayami, Kaiser Permanente; Judith Hibbard, University of Oregon; Holly Jimison, Oregon Health Sciences University; Diana Jones, Oregon Health Policy Institute and Oregon Health Plan Administrator's Office; David Lansky, Foundation for Accountability; Cindi McElhaney, Physician Association of Clackamas County Health Plan; Scott Page, NW Surgical Associates; David Phillips, Oregon Health Sciences University; Pia Schneider, Blue Cross/Blue Shield of Oregon; Paul Sher, Oregon

Health Sciences University; and Dan Stevens, Center for Outcomes Research and Education.

Members of the *consumer committee* were Becky Adelman, consumer-at-large; Sue Burlison, Office of Medical Assistance Programs; Gloria Colton, consumer-at-large; Ruben Contreras, consumer-at-large; Pat Gardner, consumer-at-large; Vickie Gates, Oregon Health Plan Administrator; Lew Parker, consumer-at-large; Sandra Spiegel, consumer-at-large; Len Torvinen, consumer-at-large; Nicholas Wickliff, consumer-at-large; and Mylia Wray, Benova, Inc.

Finally, we pay particular tribute to Peter Kohler, M.D., president of the Oregon Health Sciences University, and to Judith Ramaley, Ph.D., former president of Portland State University for having the vision and clarity of intent that spawned the Oregon Health Policy Institute in 1993 to serve as an academic resource to policymakers in the state of Oregon.

P.P.H.
M.R.G.

The Editors

Pamela P. Hanes is an associate professor of public health and preventive medicine and associate director of the Oregon Health Policy Institute at the Oregon Health Sciences University in Portland, Oregon. Hanes earned her B.S. in sociology of the family at West Virginia University, Morgantown (1974), her M.S.W. in health policy and administration from California State University at Sacramento (1987), and her Ph.D. in social welfare policy from the University of California, Berkeley (1989). Before joining the School of Medicine faculty at the Oregon Health Sciences University, she was on the faculty in the School of Social Work at the University of Wisconsin, Madison.

Hanes has worked in the field of health policy, health services research, and health program evaluation for the past twenty-five years, analyzing health policies from a variety of vantage points, including service as a principal consultant on health and welfare to the California Assembly Ways and Means Committee, as a program developer and project evaluator for three private foundations in the San Francisco Bay Area, and as an academically based health services researcher and scholar at the University of California, San Francisco, in addition to her tenure in Madison and Portland. Hanes's main research interests have focused on state policy formulation as it relates to access to quality care for vulnerable and otherwise disenfranchised populations. She has conducted numerous studies in the areas of health and disability policy, identifying and analyzing nonfinancial barriers to health care access and measuring the impact of managed care on children with special health care needs and persons with significant physical disabilities. In her research, Hanes has focused on the experience of health and medical care from a consumer perspective. Issues related to the influence of culture, ethnicity, and individual differences have received special emphasis in her work.

Merwyn R. Greenlick is a professor and is chair of the Department of Public Health and Preventive Medicine, School of Medicine, Oregon Health Sciences University. He was, until July 1995, director of the Kaiser Permanente Center for Health Research and vice president for research, Kaiser Foundation Hospitals. Greenlick received his B.S. in pharmacy and his M.S. in pharmacy administration from Wayne State University in Detroit, Michigan, and his Ph.D. in medical care organization from the University of Michigan, with specializations in sociology, social psychology, and research design.

Greenlick has served as research adviser to many projects throughout the country and as an adviser to several foreign government research and medical care projects. He was elected to the Institute of Medicine (IOM) of the National Academy of Sciences in 1971. He has served on a number of IOM study committees and chairs the IOM's committee on community-based drug treatment. He has served on a variety of National Institutes of Health review panels, including the health services development panel. Greenlick was a senior fellow at the Center for Advanced Study in the Behavioral Sciences at Stanford during 1995–96. He currently serves as an adviser to the chair and CEO of the Kaiser Foundation Health Plan.

Greenlick's research has been in the areas of large-scale demonstration projects relating to the organization and financing of medical care and behavioral interventions in disease prevention. He was a co-principal investigator for the Medicare Prospective Payment Demonstration Project ("Medicare Plus"), which provided care to over 7,600 Medicare beneficiaries on a capitation basis. He is currently the principal investigator of the Kaiser Permanente site of the Social HMO Project, which is investigating the financial feasibility of providing a comprehensive range of long-term care services for the frail elderly.

In addition to his work with large-scale demonstrations, Green-lick has had extensive experience in clinical trials, both at the local and national levels, and has provided considerable leadership at the national level. He was a principal investigator in the Dietary Inter-vention Study in Children (DISC) and is chair of DISC's national design and analysis committee National Heart, Lung, and Blood Institute of the National Institutes of Health (NHLBI).

Greenlick is a distinguished fellow of the Association for Health Services Research and in 1994 received the association's President's Award for his lifetime contributions to the field.

The Contributors

Barry F. Anderson is a professor of psychology at Portland State University. He earned his B.A. (1957) in psychology at Stanford University and his Ph.D. (1963) in experimental psychology at Johns Hopkins University. He is a member of the Society for Judgment and Decision Making, the American Psychological Society, and the American Psychological Association.

Anderson's interests lie in the area of decision psychology, with an emphasis on applications. He has published a number of papers and the following books: *The Psychology Experiment*, second edition (1971), *Cognitive Psychology: The Study of Knowing, Learning, and Thinking* (1975), *The Complete Thinker* (1980), and (with several coauthors) *Concepts in Judgment and Decision Research* (1981).

Anderson has developed decision processes for the U.S. Bureau of Reclamation, the U.S. Fish and Wildlife Service, the Rocky Flats Monitoring Committee, the Oregon Children's Injury Prevention Program, the Oregon Health Services Commission, Oregon Health Decisions, the Oregon Health Sciences University School of Nursing, the Portland Bureau of Housing, the Multnomah County Commissioners, and others.

Christine Edlund earned her B.S. in sociology from the University of Oregon (1973) and her M.A. in urban studies from Portland State University (1977). Edlund has worked for the last eighteen years in the field of survey research, program evaluation, and, more recently, health services research. She has consulted privately and in the Office of Medical Assistance Programs (Oregon Health Plan), as well as in the Providence Health System. She has designed and implemented a comprehensive program evaluation for Oregon's Medicaid managed care delivery system. The program developed for the Oregon Health Plan's Medicaid population included client satisfaction and health status surveys, as well as particular HEDIS measures, utilization rates, and various qualitative measures. Edlund's expertise is in the development and implementation of survey research tools, as well as the design and implementation of program evaluations.

Edlund is currently a senior research analyst with the Center for Outcomes Research and Education (CORE) at Providence Health Systems. Her responsibilities include the development and implementation of various survey research programs assessing patient, physician, and employee satisfaction as part of an overall program of accountability and quality improvement initiatives.

Michael J. Garland is professor and vice chair of the Department of Public Health and Preventive Medicine and director of educational policy in the Center for Medical Ethics at the Oregon Health Sciences University. He earned his B.A. (1961) in philosophy and letters at St. Louis University, his M.A. (1968) in theology at Notre Dame University, and the *docteur ès sciences réligieuses* (1971) from the University of Strasbourg in France.

Garland's main research activity is in the field of social ethics and health policy, with particular focus on the public's role in the development, implementation, and evaluation of health policy. He has published widely in the field of biomedical ethics, focusing on issues related to the allocation of health care resources, social ethics education in health professions' curricula, ethics in human experimentation, ethical issues in withholding treatment from the terminally ill, and the community's role in guiding ethical choices in health policy. Garland cofounded Oregon Health Decisions in 1983 to foster public participation in the development of state health policy. The organization has played a continuing role in maintaining public involvement in critical policy choices affecting the Oregon Health Plan.

Garland is chair-elect of American Health Decisions, a national umbrella organization of state groups committed to fostering public participation in health policy. He is also co-chair of the Oregon Medicaid Advisory Committee, serves on the Insurance Pool Governing Board, and is chair of the Oregon Health Division's Institutional Review Board.

Bruce W. Goldberg is an associate professor in the Department of Public Health and Preventive Medicine and the Department of Family Medicine at Oregon Health Sciences University School of Medicine. He earned his M.D. degree (1982) from the Mount Sinai School of Medicine in New York City and completed a residency in family practice at Duke University in 1985.

Goldberg is the associate medical director of CareOregon, a Medicaid-only managed care organization that is a partnership between county health departments, community health centers, and an academic medical center. His professional and scholarly interests include the organization and delivery of health services to medically underserved populations, clinical quality improvement, population-based health services, and firearm violence prevention.

Daniel M. Harris has been the director of Oregon's Health Resources Commission since its inception in early 1992, and he led the commission in its development and implementation of the Medical Technology Assessment Program, part of the state's efforts to improve the quality and contain the cost of health care. He is also a member of the professional staff of the Office for Oregon Health Plan Policy and Research, where he actively participates in that office's efforts to develop a comprehensive database of Oregon's health system and its performance, including a consumer-oriented scorecard.

Prior to assuming his position with the state of Oregon, Harris was vice president of planning with Legacy Health System in Portland, Oregon, and director of market research, program development, and strategic planning with its predecessor system, HealthLink. Among other innovations he introduced while at Legacy/HealthLink, Harris developed a patient satisfaction monitoring program as part of the system's quality, value, and service initiative.

Harris earned a Ph.D. in medical and organizational sociology from the State University of New York at Stony Brook in 1972. Before assuming his duties in Portland in 1984, he was an assistant professor of health services administration at the University of Missouri in Columbia, Missouri, and an assistant professor of sociology at Case Western Reserve University in Cleveland, Ohio, and Hollins College in Roanoke, Virginia. He has written, published, and presented numerous professional, governmental, and management papers and reports in the areas of health care delivery, health policy, patient behavior, consumer satisfaction, and medical technology assessment. He currently teaches in Oregon's multicampus master of public health program as a clinical associate professor at Oregon Health Sciences University and is an adjunct associate professor at Portland State University. He is also a research affiliate with the Oregon Health Policy Institute and was part of the institute staff that supported the early work of the Oregon Consumer Scorecard Consortium during 1994–96.

Holly B. Jimison is an assistant professor in the Department of Public Health and Preventive Medicine, with a joint appointment in medical informatics at Oregon Health Sciences University. She also directs the Informed Patient Decisions Group in research on methods for enhancing patient participation in decisions about their health care. She received a B.S. in mathematics (1973) from the University of Illinois and a Ph.D. in medical informatics (1990) from Stanford University, with thesis work on using computer models to tailor patient education materials.

Jimison's main research activities have focused on both the formative and summative evaluations of consumer health information systems. She has developed and piloted new methods for assessing patient preferences, communicating risk information, and automating tailored explanations of computer decision models. She has published several articles on consumer health informatics and the research issues associated with the field.

Jimison currently serves on a federal government–sponsored Science Panel for the Evaluation of Consumer Health Information Technologies and is on the board of the Oregon Consumer Health Alliance.

H. Diana Jones is an executive analyst with the Office of Oregon Health Plan Policy and Research. Jones earned her B.S. (1975) in business administration and her M.S. in public administration at the University of Missouri, Columbia. Before joining Oregon state government, Jones was director of strategic planning at Saint Luke's health system in Kansas City, Missouri.

Jones's primary research interests have focused on the development of performance measurement tools for consumers of health care. She served as the project coordinator for the Oregon Consumer Scorecard Project and in that role, supervised the production of the prototype scorecard materials. Jones is currently responsible for organizing the next phase of scorecard development work in Oregon under the auspices of the Office of the Oregon Health Plan Policy and Research. She will be working with the reconstituted Oregon Consumer Scorecard Consortium on the development, demonstration, and evaluation of a range of performance measurement tools for managed health insurance organizations.

Grading Health Care

Chapter One

Reporting Quality in a Market-Driven Health Care System

Daniel M. Harris and Pamela P. Hanes

Prior to the fall of 1994, it was generally assumed that government-sponsored or government-mandated initiatives would create the impetus to achieve the policy objectives that Americans wanted from their health care system. But this expectation ended, at least for the time being, with the defeat of the Clinton administration's health reform proposal and the November 1994 midterm congressional elections. Clearly, health care reform is more likely to be played out in the competitive marketplace than in the halls of the U.S. Congress. Leadership in health systems reform has largely shifted to the private sector; government now plays a partnership role—guiding and facilitating but no longer directing reform efforts. Recent initiatives in consumer health care scorecards must be viewed in this context. Although the federal government has recently enacted some health insurance and balanced budget reforms, these actions were not aimed at structural reform. Rather, they sought to bring more individuals into the health care market and reform the payment mechanisms within that market.

This chapter provides a public policy framework for evaluating the efficacy of consumer health care scorecard efforts and to locate the Oregon experience within this framework. Health care report cards have been variously defined. Report cards have been developed mostly for major purchasers of health care; that is, large employers and federal and state governments. These group purchasers presumably will use report cards to compare health plans based on cost and quality and will thereby purchase the best value

1

for the dollars invested. Quality indicators have tended to be consumer satisfaction ratings (for example, access to care, interpersonal communications with physicians, and access to specialist referrals), process of care outcomes (rates of fully immunized two-year-olds and annual mammography rates for women over fifty years of age), and clinical outcomes (CABG maternity rates).

For our purposes, the operational definition of a consumer health care scorecard was a document that would provide comparative qualitative and quantitative performance information, highlighting meaningful differences between health plans. The primary function of such a scorecard would be to inform the choice decision-making process of *individual* consumers.

After outlining the public policy context that helped spawn the scorecard movement, we will review and discuss the policy functions that have been proposed for consumer scorecards and the potential barriers to achieving these policy objectives. We will highlight some experiences from the Oregon Consumer Scorecard Consortium to illustrate the lessons we learned. Finally, in an epilogue, we will provide an update on several recent policy developments in Oregon that are related to scorecard development.

Chapter Two sets the stage for the development of a consumer scorecard, elucidating the work plan and specifying the policy context in Oregon. Subsequent chapters will discuss how the Oregon Consumer Scorecard Consortium set about learning what Oregon consumers wanted to know about health plan performance and quality, their preferences for having this information presented, lessons learned from the measurement and reporting challenges encountered along the way, and the extent to which these lessons can be generalized and applied to other settings and used with other populations.

Public Policy Context

Health policy in the United States for several decades has emphasized the tripartite goals of ensuring equitable access to quality health care at an acceptable and affordable cost. These goals were clearly articulated in the National Health Planning and Resources Development Act of 1974 (PL 93–641), which stated that "the achievement of equal access to quality health care at a reasonable cost is a priority of the federal government." Similarly, Oregon's enabling legislation implementing PL 93–641 in 1977 stated that "the achievement of reasonable access to quality health care at a reasonable cost is a priority of the State of Oregon" (Oregon Revised Statutes, Chapter 442.025[1]). More recently, the 1993 Oregon Legislative Assembly restated this policy as the basis of the Oregon Health Plan, "[I]t is the intention of the Legislative Assembly to achieve the goals of universal access to an adequate level of high quality health care at an affordable cost" (Oregon Revised Statutes, Chapter 414.018[1]).

Although these three policy objectives have at times been in direct conflict with each other (Kissick, 1994, pp. 2–4), one objective has been emphasized more frequently than the others. Taken together, they have formed the basis of U.S. health policy for at least the past quarter century and most likely will continue to guide public action into the next century.

If these policy objectives are ever to be achieved simultaneously, the question of *how* to achieve them will need to be addressed. In the past, three devices have been used: (1) *internal control mechanisms* or self-regulation on the part of the health care industry through professional ethics, licensing boards, accreditation and certification of programs, staff, and institutions, and peer review efforts; (2) *external control mechanisms* primarily through government regulation and mandates; and (3) *market mechanisms* whereby the invisible hand of the market, in the form of competitive market forces and economic self-interest, is deliberately extended to motivate all parties to make individual decisions that will collectively achieve public policy objectives.

Although these three devices need not be mutually exclusive and can work together in concert, they often produce more cacophony than harmony. In practice, it has usually been the case that one sector dominates center stage at any given time.

During the first half of this century, professionally driven control mechanisms predominated. This period of professional dominance was followed by several decades of aggressive governmental involvement—both legislative and bureaucratic—in the various arenas where health systems design and development activities occurred (Starr, 1982). Most recently, especially after the demise of President Clinton's health care reform efforts, the private market has increasingly been the mechanism of choice for expanding access, improving quality, and containing the overall costs of health care. The implicit justification for relying on the market is that government cannot, and health professionals will not, achieve these three policy objectives if left to their own devices.

This does not mean that government and the professions have no roles left to play. On the contrary, both sectors continue to be actively involved in health care reform efforts. However, the systems reform solution of choice embraced by government officials, health care providers, and volume purchasers of health care is a dynamic health care marketplace (see Herzlinger, 1997). Rather than directly managing, controlling, or regulating health care delivery, the reform strategies of the late 1990s are to support the private sector through various incentives and opportunities, thereby permitting the market to shape and direct professional and managerial behavior, particularly in the areas of access, quality, and cost (Enthoven and Kronick, 1991; Teisberg, Porter, and Brown, 1994; Stoline and Weiner, 1993; and Zelman, 1996).

Competitive Markets

According to economic theory, for competitive markets to fulfill these multiple functions, a number of conditions must be met, including the condition that sufficient numbers of motivated, informed, value-sensitive buyers and sellers must exist and that none should unfairly dominate the market. Additionally, each player must have an adequate knowledge of market conditions and be willing and able to act rationally on what they know. In theory, if these necessary conditions are met, the supply of health care should come into equilibrium with demand and be available at the best price without sacrificing quality.

However, as numerous health care economists have previously noted, the conditions necessary for achieving this market equilibrium are either missing or inadequate in health care markets (Teisberg, Porter, and Brown, 1994; Feldstein, 1993; Roemer and Roemer, 1982; Ginzberg, 1996; and Wilkerson, Devers, and Given, 1997). What we have historically experienced in the health care sector is chronic market failure. Factors contributing to this failure include (1) the asymmetry of information and power between health care providers or suppliers and the consumers or purchasers of health care, (2) the inability of buyers or consumers to adequately differentiate among providers on the basis of quality and value, and (3) the insulating effect of third-party insurance that masks the true cost of care for both providers and consumers, making price sensitivity a moot issue. In these circumstances government, acting in the public interest, seeks to create the necessary conditions to protect consumers from the consequences of a failed market.

We now are witnessing the emergence of publicly sponsored initiatives in the area of consumer information, including the development of consumer scorecards. Such consumer education and empowerment initiatives in health care ought to be examined in light of government's historic role of preventing market failure and, failing that, of protecting the public when it occurs. With this role in mind, the ideal function of a consumer scorecard from a public policy perspective would be to foster the necessary conditions for a competitive health care market to operate and to monitor the ongoing performance of this market. The success or failure of consumer scorecards must then be measured against the degree to which they contribute to achieving the public policy goals of increasing access, improving quality, and controlling costs.

Policy Role of Consumer Scorecards

Given this framework, the potential public policy functions of a consumer scorecard are many (Gold and Woolridge, 1995). With each potential role, a practical question lingers:

- Can scorecards reliably measure and report health plan and provider quality and performance?
- Will scorecards produce an informed cadre of market-savvy consumers?
- Can scorecards foster the market conditions required to achieve the policy goals of increased access, high quality, and reasonable costs?
- Why is the development of consumer scorecards of such interest to the federal government that the Agency for Health Care Policy and Research (AHCPR) is sponsoring a five-year Consumer Assessment of Health Plans Survey (CAHPS) Project?

Asymmetry of Information

Consumer scorecards can be one mechanism by which to address the information asymmetry that currently exists in the health care marketplace (Gaus and Fraser, 1996). As noted earlier, competitive markets fail, among other reasons, when buyers and sellers do not have sufficient knowledge about the prices, quantity, and quality of competing goods and services. Gaining this knowledge may well increase the potential for rational, prudent purchasing decisions related to buying health care.

Comparative health plan performance reports are being proposed as one way to address the information needs shared by both individual consumers and volume purchasers. If successful, scorecards have the potential to redress some of the imbalance in information that currently exists between consumers and purchasers on the one hand and health plans and providers on the other.

A closely related function and promise of scorecards is that of ensuring that competitive products are based at least as much on quality, value, and service as they are on cost. In the absence of reliable information on quality, including clinical processes, outcomes, and service measures, consumers and purchasers will be forced to base their health care decisions largely on cost. By providing comparative information on clinical quality, service, and value and by encouraging the use of such information, scorecards may well increase the likelihood that the highest quality of health care can be purchased at competitive prices.

Access

Although discussions about access often focus on its financial aspects (for example, access to affordable health insurance coverage), other dimensions of access are equally important. These include consideration of culturally and socially acceptable services, the availability of a range of providers and facilities, and the availability of other enabling services that facilitate access, including extended office hours and the availability of child care.

Another purpose of health care scorecards is to provide comparative information to consumers about health plan performance in the area of access, especially as determined from a consumer perspective. This information would allow consumers to act in an informed manner when selecting health plans and providers, and it would also help ensure that health plans pay attention to these dimensions of access when designing their networks, policies, and procedures, thereby ensuring maximum accessibility of plan benefits and services.

Quality

The measurement of health care quality has two important dimensions: (1) objective measures of clinical performance such as outcomes of treatment, including restoration of function, and (2) the

more subjective measures that include patients' self-reported perceptions of the quality of care provided. Health plan scorecards
have the potential to reliably report both dimensions of quality.

Consumer assessments of health care, particularly as reported
through the experiential lenses of heavy users, have the potential
to promote plan accountability in powerful ways, thereby shaping
the market as theorists suggest it should be shaped.

In this capacity, health plan scorecards can provide a critical
feedback loop from consumers to health plans to providers. Consumer feedback should include what patients want that they aren't
getting in the way of service, how satisfied or dissatisfied they are
with the services provided, and how each plan is performing relative to its competitors in the same market. This information would
allow plans to close the accountability loop by sharing this information with providers they contract with for services.

Other Scorecard Functions

Comparative health plan scorecard information can also be used by
volume purchasers—public and private employers and public benefit programs—so that each can function as a more prudent buyer
in the health care marketplace. Scorecards that include enrollee
assessments of health plan and provider quality, access, and service
performance, even if designed for an individual consumer audience,
will provide valuable information to those who would purchase
health benefits on their behalf.

Reliably reported consumer satisfaction information can ensure
that purchasers take their employees' or beneficiaries' (in the case
of public benefit programs) values and preferences into account.
This *user quality audit* provides a mechanism for purchasers to monitor the acceptability of plan offerings and to bring market pressure
to bear on plans that fail to adequately satisfy their members.

Even if all this information is made available to consumers, the
market will probably not perform as expected with input from indi-

vidual consumers alone. Health care scorecards can help in this case as well. By providing a source of information to sponsors who purchase health benefits, private organizations working to improve health care quality, and government agencies responsible for protecting the public interest, periodic, independently published scorecards can effectively monitor health plan performance in ways that can help "correct" the market. Scorecards can provide an incentive for improving market performance or can inform government regulation when markets fail.

Because makers of public policy are increasingly looking to managed care as the most promising means of expanding access, containing costs, and improving the quality of health care, another purpose of scorecards should be to foster greater understanding of managed care principles to consumers while ensuring that providers are responsive to consumer needs and preferences. For managed health care plans to be the instruments many policymakers intend them to be, it is critical that consumers be fully informed and able to optimize the benefits derived from these complex systems of care. Optimizing benefits includes knowing how to access and use preventive services and how and when to rely on primary, secondary, and specialized care providers. Having the informational tools to know how and when to insist that medical care needs are met in a timely fashion is also important.

Scorecards are also being promoted for purposes not directly related to correcting market imbalances. For example, in Oregon they were primarily conceived to be a choice tool to help individual consumers select a health plan that best meets their health care needs and preferences. Similarly, Oregon's scorecard development included providing comparative *navigational* information that would help consumers find their way through the managed care maze by delineating the ways in which various plans *manage care*.

Finally, scorecards have been proposed as a source of information for health plans to use in their internal quality control and continuous quality improvement programs. This function can be viewed as a benefit as long as internal use promotes meaningful quality improvement activities and not simply the manipulation of scores that can then be used for marketing purposes.

Potential Barriers to Achieving Policy Goals

Given the various, though generally interrelated, policy objectives proposed for consumer scorecards, a number of potentially problematic issues need to be recognized and addressed early in the scorecard development process. Resolution of these issues requires that all stakeholders involved participate actively in the development of the scorecard instrument.

Multiple Objectives

It is unlikely that all conceivable policy objectives can be equally or even adequately achieved in a single scorecard instrument. Depending on the breadth and nature of stakeholder involvement, some objectives will be secondary to others and might better be achieved through other means. In Oregon, one of the first formal actions taken by the consortium steering committee was to make explicit the purpose and function of the scorecard to be developed and to agree to five criteria that would guide the selection of measures to be included on it. The purpose was to create a consumer scorecard that would serve as a choice tool for enrollees in the Oregon Health Plan. The five criteria that measures would need to meet, in order of importance were:

1. The measure should have demonstrated utility from a consumer perspective.
2. The burden of collecting the data generated by the measure should be minimized for health plans as much as possible.
3. The measure should have high reliability and validity.
4. The measure should enhance understanding of managed care and the dimensions of quality that can be measured.

5. The measure should provide feedback to consumers on community health improvement resulting from health plan performance monitoring.

If several instruments are warranted, it would then be necessary to ensure that each is consistent enough in data collection, analytic approach, and indicator definition that the credibility and soundness of the overall project is not compromised.

Multiple Audiences

Scorecards should empower and give voice to consumers. But many questions remain as to whether they can do so in a way that will cause health plans to respond to the concerns that consumers voice. Various audiences and needs must be satisfied through a scorecard effort, and many subpopulations of consumers have differing information needs. Scorecard definitions will vary as to how quality or satisfaction should be measured and reported. How each voice gets heard on a given scorecard is a challenge yet to be resolved.

Given consumers' preference for health plan information that is tailored to their own health and situation, it may not be possible to produce a single scorecard that reports information in the level of detail that is meaningful and useful to all consumers. Substantial costs and methodological challenges are involved in collecting and reporting specific, tailored information. Therefore, scorecards may be but one tool in a larger information kit.

Scorecards as Tools of Change

If health care performance is to be improved through the use of scorecards as envisioned by policymakers, the information supplied to consumers and group purchasers must address the current information imbalance. For their part, health plans must be prepared to be responsive to scorecard results, accept the legitimacy of the tool, and act responsibly. Many fear that health plans will simply learn how to "game" the scores in order to look good on a comparative scorecard through nonsubstantive, cosmetic changes. A health plan could, for example, improve its ratings on a consumer scorecard, not by improving service but by refusing to enroll consumers who could be categorized as whiners, complainers, or troublemakers. Thus, instead of improving access and quality for groups of vulnerable consumers, scorecards could exacerbate their problems in important performance areas.

Scorecard developers should be aware that this possibility exists and take steps to avoid it. One possible solution is to build risk-adjustment factors into the analytic plan developed for reporting consumer satisfaction data. These factors would play the same role as those developed for health care utilization, which is to adjust capitation rates upward for plans that serve disproportionately sicker populations. In the same way that risk adjustment provides a fiscal incentive to health plans that enroll sicker members, satisfaction adjustment factors might reduce the likelihood that plans will avoid enrolling these populations to achieve higher satisfaction scores.

Teaching to the Test

Another strategy that should be anticipated is teaching to the test. This is happening when those who are being evaluated (health plans) alter their behavior over time to conform to the evaluation instrument (scorecard). This is similar to teachers who are being evaluated on how well their students perform on a standardized test focusing their efforts on preparing students to do well on the test. Scorecard developers should consider the likely effects of performing to the scorecard. What would happen if health plans and providers changed their behavior only to improve their scores on a scorecard? Would this behavior lead to real improvements in quality, value, and service?

Gaming the Score

Somewhat related to teaching to the test is gaming the score. This occurs when health plans deliberately avoid change while appearing to improve performance. One option for avoiding this scenario is to rotate the quality, access, and satisfaction measures that are included on a scorecard on a periodic basis. By so doing, health plans will need to be attentive to a sufficiently broad range of performance measures to minimize the temptation to participate in this game.

Paternalism Versus Education

Some would argue that consumers are not adequately informed, aware, or able to act in their own best interest when it comes to judging quality and choosing a health plan. If this is the case, scorecards might be constructed to educate consumers about what they *should* know, as opposed to what they say they want to know to make an informed choice. Or perhaps professionals should act in the best interests of consumers, basing their actions on expert opinion, clinical outcomes, and effectiveness research. Assuming that this does not represent a false dichotomy, paternalism becomes a real issue for scorecard developers.

In Oregon, there is an ongoing debate as to whether it is advisable to bring these two perspectives together over time. This might occur through a consumer education campaign intended to shape consumers' preferences for information based on expert opinion of what an informed consumer is, what information is needed to be informed, and how to make the best use of this information when making choices.

A related issue is that many clinical quality indicators that experts consider important are not viewed similarly by consumers. For example, consumers have reported population-based performance measures as either irrelevant or of little utility when assessing a health plan (Hibbard and Jewett, 1996; Edgeman-Levitan and Cleary, 1996). There are a number of reasons for this. For one, many people assume that competence is ensured through professional education and training, credentialing by specialty boards, hospitals and health plan accreditation, and the licensing of health care professionals and facilities.

Given the mystique surrounding technical measures of clinical quality—a mystique shared by health professionals and consumers alike—many consumers rightfully acknowledge that they do not know how to interpret these indicators when they are presented for informational purposes. Consumers have also reported that they would not hold a health plan accountable for its performance relative to certain population-based clinical measures such as mammography rates or smoking cessation program participation because use of these services is too strongly influenced by individual attitudes and behaviors (Hibbard and Jewett, 1996). Likewise, some consumers will hold their individual provider accountable for health outcomes as opposed to their health plan.

Similarly, population-based clinical quality measures are not relevant to the large majority of consumers who are generally in good health, who don't use health care very often, or who use it mostly for nonacute or self-limiting conditions. These consumers are more interested in service quality. This suggests that clinical quality measures should be tailored to those who use health care services the most, that is, individuals with chronic health conditions or acute illnesses. Such individuals, or those at risk of becoming so, want the option of going outside their health plan's provider network to get what they think is the best care available. This has contributed to the growing popularity of "point-of-service" plans (Zelman, 1996) and the estimated 15–20 percent of managed care enrollees who use providers outside their plan's network (Davis, Collins, Schoen, and Morris, 1995).

All of this suggests that if policymakers want to foster improvements in clinical quality through market dynamics, clinical quality must be a competitive factor among health plans. To do this, scorecard developers must design measures that reflect the experiences of those who are the most frequent users of services, which means that developers of clinical quality measures must ensure that questions have meaning and relevance both to individual consumers and group purchasers (Moskowitz, 1997).

Community Health Improvement

A final concern to be addressed in scorecard development is the relationship between medical care and health improvement. In the context of scorecards, should the primary purpose of a scorecard be to improve market conditions so that the policy goals of access, cost, and quality can be achieved? Or should it be to monitor health improvement in the population? There is an assumed link between these two goals.

In Oregon, as noted earlier, the policy objective of the Oregon Health Plan was to achieve universal access to an adequate level of quality health care at an affordable cost. However, as expressed more recently (in March of 1996) by the Health Care Agenda Working Group in a set of recommendations to Governor Kitzhaber, "The primary goal of the health care system must be to maintain and improve the health of Oregonians." It remains to be seen whether the consumer scorecard currently under development will have the positive impact on health improvement envisioned by its framers.

Lessons Learned from the Oregon Experience

Many of the questions raised in this chapter were confronted in the development of the consumer scorecard prototype developed by the consortium. Chapter Four discusses in detail the messages that were delivered by focus group participants as we sought to learn what consumers want and need if they are to be informed purchasers. Summarized next is the content of these messages within the political and economic framework outlined in this chapter.

• For scorecards to have the potential for success in a market-driven health care system, it is essential that all affected stakeholders be present at the table, that they meaningfully participate in the process, and that, at some level, consensus is achieved as to the objectives and means to pursue them.

• Technical expertise in the measurement, analysis, and presentation of data is integral to the utility of the final scorecard project. It is naive to believe that scorecards with integrity can be produced without this expertise.

• If public policy makers want to foster competition based on quality and value and not solely on cost, then it is imperative that those who exert this competitive pressure on health plans—individual consumers and volume purchasers—must understand the meaning of clinical quality measurement and use it accordingly.

• The scorecard development process requires a neutral, legitimate, and well-respected independent entity to function in a staff capacity to providers, health plans, consumers, and purchasers to keep everyone at the table and "keep the process honest." There must be accountability in both the methods used and acceptance of the outputs produced.

• It will be difficult, and likely not possible, to satisfy all potential interests, needs, and purposes in a single scorecard instrument. As a result, it is essential to prioritize goals and agree to the priorities that are established. This is a political process and, as such, requires political skills.

• Quality is in the eyes of the beholder. What is considered to be an appropriate measure of quality varies widely among the affected constituencies. So saying, it will be necessary to clearly and specifically define the target audience, fully understand the meanings they give to quality, and then determine how these meanings can be quantified and reported.

Conclusion

Health plan performance measurement can be translated into consumer scorecards but not without considerable attention to process and methods. The promise is great that scorecards can be tools that truly inform and empower individual consumers to make better choices based on objective and subjective measures of quality and value. They also hold potential to be quality feedback tools for consumers who can legitimately express their quality concerns through a vehicle to which a response is an expectation of all concerned.

Scorecards can also be used as instruments of public policy to harness competitive market forces and thereby achieve public policy objectives. As such, they will provide market incentives for the structural reform of health care delivery, improve quality at the population level (both clinical quality and service-related), hold health care providers and plans accountable to payors (consumers, purchasers, and the public sector), and ultimately improve the performance of providers and of plans.

To educate American health care consumers in the utility of comparative health plan information requires a deliberative and iterative process. Health care consumers are neither used to making informed choices nor have they had access to independent third parties to help them evaluate and then choose a plan that is best for them. Nevertheless, the promise remains that over time, scorecards can be developed to achieve important, consensus-driven public policy goals in a market-driven health care system.

Epilogue: Recent Developments in Oregon

There have been two developments in Oregon since the completion of the prototype development work that are noteworthy from a public policy perspective. The first of these was the passage of SB 21 (Chapter 343, Oregon Laws, 1997). This legislation significantly revised and expanded previously enacted patients' bill of rights statutes and codified consumer protections in the area of health insurance. It is interesting to note that in spite of the intentionality of voluntariness undergirding the consortium's effort, the legislature and governor found it necessary to set in place a detailed mandatory reporting system for health insurers to follow.

This legislation includes various sections related to consumers' right to know about their health plans' benefits, coverage, and policies and procedures for managing health care. The provisions reflect the many messages that consumers provided to us during the numerous focus groups held in conjunction with scorecard development.

Specifically, the bill requires that all health insurers offering a health benefit plan in the state shall have written policies that recognize the rights of enrollees to (1) voice grievances, (2) be provided information about the organization, its services, and providers, (3) participate in decision making regarding their health care, and (4) be treated with respect and have their need for privacy recognized. The legislation goes on to specify a detailed set of requirements for information disclosure, producing information "in plain language," standards for timeliness, appeals processes, provisions for referrals and after-hours care, and so forth. Most relevant to the scorecard effort are the provisions that require insurers to make available annual reports of grievances, insurers' risk-sharing arrangements with physicians and other providers, and the ways health insurers monitor and improve quality of care. Finally, for insurers who offer a managed health insurance product, the requirements become even more detailed regarding quality assurance monitoring and reporting.

SB 21 also directs the Office for Oregon Health Plan Policy and Research (formerly the Office of the Health Plan Administrator) to reconstitute the consortium. It should be composed of interested parties to (1) develop, on a voluntary basis, standardized, quantitative performance measures for use by consumers, purchasers, and providers to continuously assess the clinical and service-related quality of the health care arranged for or provided by managed health insurance organizations; (2) encourage managed health insurance organizations to collect, on a voluntary basis, these performance measures and share that information with the consortium; and (3) develop, test, refine, and produce one or more managed health care performance scorecards to provide consumers and purchasers with comparisons of managed health insurance organizations with respect to organizational characteristics, clinical and service-related quality, and member and patient satisfaction.

The office has been mandated to report to the 1999 Legislative Assembly on the accomplishments of the consortium and to make recommendations regarding the need for further statutory direction. The report will include a recommendation on the feasibility of implementing a statewide enrollee satisfaction survey to be administered by the Oregon Department of Business and Consumer Affairs Insurance Division.

The legislation is an interesting step beyond the initial charge to begin a process of consumer scorecard development for enrollees in the Oregon Health Plan. The scope of participating stakeholders has been broadened to include major health care purchasers in the state. It is also significantly more directive than the two sentences contained in the 1993 statute that spawned the original Oregon Consumer Scorecard Consortium. The charge to the newly forming consortium is more explicit, and the scope of performance measurement is more clearly specified.

Although still described as a voluntary effort, the terms of the effort, as well as the consequences of not achieving consensus, are more forcefully articulated in SB 21. The addition of state agency representatives beyond those involved in the initial consortium activities are a signal to the provider community that this truly is a public-private partnership activity.

The second development in Oregon has been the creation of an Oregon Health Care Purchasers Coalition. The coalition is not a purchasing alliance or cooperative but a voluntary coalition of public and private employers and the state Medicaid agency, which formed in response to the common set of purchasing issues each entity faces. Among these issues are those of defining and measuring quality and value across insurers and providers and the desire to address definitional issues jointly and cooperatively rather than separately and competitively. The coalition represents large employers in Oregon, as well as a purchasing cooperative of small employers organized by Associated Oregon Industries (AOI), a business trade organization.

A major priority of the coalition is continuing the work of the consortium in scorecard development, specifically, in producing standardized performance measures and information for their collective use as well as that of their employees. The AOI purchasing cooperative, *HealthChoice*, will be a test site for the federally sponsored Consumers Assessment of Health Plans Survey and will work with health plans and providers to develop and pilot-test clinical outcome performance measures.

Resources

The federal government is seeking to provide information to health care consumers through several mechanisms in addition to scorecards. Two recent examples of this effort include (1) the recent release of *PubMed*, a public access MedLine capability on the Internet at the National Library of Medicine website (http://www.ncbi.nlm.nih.gov/pubmed); (2) the *Healthfinder* website, which is "a gateway consumer health and human services information" website from the federal government (http://www.healthfinder.gov).

References

Davis, K., Collins, K. S., Schoen, C., and Morris, C. "Choice Matters: Enrollees' Views of Their Health Plans." *Health Affairs*, 1995, 14(2), 99–112.

Edgeman-Levitan, S., and Cleary, P. "What Information Do Consumers Want and Need?" *Health Affairs*, 1996, 15(4), 42–56.

Enthoven, A. C., and Kronick, R. "Universal Health Insurance Through Incentive Reform." *Journal of the American Medical Association*, 1991, 265(19), 2532–2536.

Feldstein, P. J. *Health Care Economics*. (4th ed.) Albany, N.Y.: Delmar, 1993.

Gaus, C. R., and Fraser, I. "Shifting Paradigms and the Role of Research." *Health Affairs*, 1996, 15(2), 235–242.

Ginzberg, E. "The Health Care Market: Theory and Reality." *Journal of the American Medical Association*, 1996, *276*(10), 777–778.

Gold, M., and Woolridge, J. "Surveying Consumer Satisfaction to Assess Managed-Care Quality: Current Practices." *Health Care Financing Review*, 1995, *16*(4), 155–173.

Herzlinger, R. *Market-Driven Health Care*. Reading, Mass.: Addison-Wesley, 1997.

Hibbard, J. H., and Jewett, J. J. "What Type of Quality Information Do Consumers Want in a Health Care Report Card?" *Medical Care Research Review*, 1996, *53*(1), 28–47.

Kissick, W. L. *Medicine's Dilemmas: Infinite Needs Versus Finite Resources*. New Haven, Conn.: Yale University Press, 1994.

Moskowitz, D. B. "Can Purchaser Report Cards Spur Competition on Quality?" *Medical Outcomes and Guidelines Alert*, Aug. 1997, pp. 5–8.

Roemer, M. I., and Roemer, J. E. "The Social Consequences of Free Trade in Health Care." *International Journal of Health Services*, 1982, *12*(1), 111–129.

Starr, P. *The Social Transformation of American Medicine*. New York: Basic Books, 1982.

Stoline, A. M., and Weiner, J. P. *The New Medical Marketplace*. (rev. ed.) Baltimore: The Johns Hopkins University Press, 1993.

Teisberg, E. O., Porter, M. E., and Brown, G. B. "Making Competition in Health Care Work." *Harvard Business Review*, July-Aug. 1994, pp. 131–141.

Wilkerson, J. D., Devers, K. J., and Given, R. S. (eds.). *Competitive Managed Care: The Emerging Health Care System*. San Francisco: Jossey-Bass, 1997.

Zelman, W. A. *The Changing Health Care Marketplace*. San Francisco: Jossey-Bass, 1996.

Chapter Two

Oregon Consortium

A Model in Scorecard Development

Pamela P. Hanes

The Oregon Health Plan Administrator was instructed by SB 5530, Statutes of 1993, to develop "a proposal for the development of a consumer scorecard that would allow the consumers of health care services under the Oregon Health Plan to obtain information concerning fees, morbidity rates generally and as related to major surgical procedures, and other factors to assist the consumer in selecting a health care provider or a health care plan."

Thus began a largely uncharted journey into the science and art of consumer scorecard development. Just as the architects of the Oregon Health Plan (OHP) had broken new ground in the design of health benefits and in lodging delivery systems in community values, the scorecard project would also prove to be groundbreaking. The project explored the information needs and preferences of health care consumers as they made choices among health plans.

The story of the Oregon Consumer Scorecard Project is one told through the voices and experiences of a voluntary consortium of public and private stakeholders in Oregon. As the debate about the appropriate role of government relative to the private marketplace continues, this book is about one state's attempt to forge an equitable, responsible, and productive partnership between potentially polarized constituencies—a partnership in pursuit of quality improvement in health care delivery.

From Work Plan to Scorecard Prototype

The original consortium represented public-private partnerships among a broad range of stakeholders in Oregon who were committed to developing a high-quality, user-friendly, consumer-oriented health plan scorecard. The primary purpose of prototype scorecard development was to aid Oregon consumers in choosing a health plan that best met their individual needs and preferences for how health care services should be delivered.

The consortium was organized to function in a nonhierarchical way, with the understanding that this flat organizational structure would maximize the participation of all members. Through a complex committee and feedback structure (steering, consumer, health plan, and technical committees), the consortium tried to ensure that all stakeholders who would benefit from or be affected by the scorecard were involved in its development. All participants made a commitment to developing an analytically and conceptually sound scorecard. Further, the scorecard would incorporate the broad range of perspectives and expertise contained in the consortium: consumers, health services researchers, clinicians, health plan representatives, and state-level policymakers.

Getting Organized

In April of 1994, two independently organized groups convened for the purpose of developing a consumer scorecard for use by OHP consumers. Subsequently, the two groups joined forces to form the Oregon Consumer Scorecard Consortium and agreed to oversee the development and implementation of a work plan to produce a prototype scorecard. Under the leadership of the Oregon Health Plan administrator, a steering committee was formed in September of 1994 to serve as the focal point for the various scorecard development activities.

To put the consortium in historical context, three activities were taking place simultaneously that laid the groundwork for the partnership: (1) the OHP administrator had been legislatively mandated in 1993 to develop a proposal for a consumer scorecard to assist OHP consumers in choosing a health plan; (2) the Oregon Office of Medical Assistance Programs (OMAP) was selected as one of seven states with a Section 1115 waiver to participate in a Medicaid HEDIS (Health Plan Employer Data and Information Set) project, sponsored by the Health Care Financing Administration (HCFA); and (3) several health plans in the private sector were in the process of releasing their own scorecards using HEDIS data as their template. Additionally, a number of academic research projects relating to consumer information needs were in various stages of submission, review, or implementation.

The policy environment in Oregon was similar to that in other states. The spark that coalesced forces and jump-started scorecard activities in Oregon, however, was the relatively abrupt transformation of its health care market from a fee-for-service delivery system to one characterized by managed care organizations. This was true for both the public and private sectors. Oregon was thus poised to tackle the underlying assumptions of competitive markets—informed consumers, accountability, and the desirability of instituting strategies to promote value in health care, including consumer scorecards.

Establishing the Approach

Through a steering committee structure, consortium members outlined the essential activities required to develop and pilot-test a prototype consumer scorecard. To begin, guiding principles were established. In retrospect, it is clear that the benefits to be derived from this approach cannot be overstated, particularly when vested interests are as divergent and the potential for conflict as great as in this situation. The process of setting forth operating assumptions by which all parties would agree to abide was an effort well worth the time involved.

Focusing on the Individual Consumer

It was agreed that the scorecard would focus on individual consumers as the end users, as opposed to private employers and public insurance sponsors who purchase health care in volume. This was an important distinction because most of the scorecard efforts at the time were not developed with this audience in mind.

Defining the Market

The legislative mandate, and therefore the focus of the original scorecard prototype development activities, was a scorecard for use by the OHP population. It was decided that the initial prototype scorecard would target the OHP-Medicaid population, as a statewide Medicaid consumer satisfaction survey was in the early stages of development at the time the consortium was formed. Although the OHP included both public and private insurance products, it did not include most insured Oregonians. Therefore, expanding the focus to all Oregon consumers was stated as a second-stage goal, once initial prototype materials had been developed and pilot-tested.

Collaborating Voluntarily

It was agreed that the scorecard would be developed as a nonregulatory collaborative effort representing both public and private interests equally. As such, considerable thought was given to the design of a committee structure that would encourage and ensure participation at all levels.

Building on Existing Knowledge

The project would use the emerging knowledge base and work of others in the area of scorecard development. At the national level, three groups were actively working in the field of consumer information and scorecard development: Research Triangle Institute (RTI), the National Committee for Quality Assurance (NCQA), and the former Group Health Association of America (GHAA), now known as the American Association of Health Plans (AAHP). The consortium staff sought to establish collegial relationships with staff from each of these organizations so that information and resource sharing between Oregon and the various projects would occur. Given the growing interest in scorecard development and the public and private groups supporting these efforts, building collaborative relationships not only would maximize individual investments but would expand knowledge in a way that isolated efforts could not.

Delineating Project Activities

The essential project activities identified by the consortium steering committee included the following:

- Knowledge building through the synthesis of existing information and secondary data analysis, as well as extracting relevant information from other projects
- Information gathering, including the identification of performance measures, collection of consumer satisfaction data, conduct of focus groups, specification of data collection protocols, and collection of data from health plans
- Prototype development through the selection of performance measures and design of alternative formats for pilot-testing measures with focus groups
- Evaluation of the prototype scorecard in focus groups for its utility among consumers, making necessary revisions, and recommending a statewide scorecard demonstration to the Oregon Health Plan administrator

Funding Scorecard Activities

Several scorecard-related projects were funded in Oregon during the prototype development process. In each case, the federal Agency for Health Care Policy and Research provided substantial resources to pursue the consortium's goals. The Computer Model as Decision

Aid project, conducted by Benova, Inc. (a Portland-based firm), used focus groups of OHP enrollees to design and pilot-test an interactive computer kiosk that would assist OHP consumers in the selection of a health plan. The Oregon Consumer Scorecard Project, staffed by faculty affiliated with the Oregon Health Policy Institute (OHPI), completed the range of activities specified for the pilot-testing of the prototype consumer scorecard. The complementarity of these two projects produced a synergistic effect, thus enhancing the final prototype scorecard developed. The one element of the work plan that remains unfunded—a statewide demonstration of the consumer scorecard—is currently under development (see the Epilogue in Chapter One).

The Oregon Consumer Scorecard Project

The project was a focused set of activities that resulted in the development and pilot-testing of a prototype consumer scorecard. The designers intended the scorecard to be responsive to the information needs of individual consumers generally and of special populations in particular, including rural residents and persons with chronic health conditions and disabilities.

A unique aspect of the Oregon project was the partnership that was established among policymakers, state agencies, private sector organizations, and the academy. The OHPI, an academically based health services research and policy analysis center in the state, was funded to serve as the staff to the consortium effort. OHPI's strategic location within the state's only health sciences university provided the necessary buffer from the politics and vested interests represented on the consortium, as well as bringing methodological rigor and science to the art of scorecard development.

Target Population

The original target population for the prototype scorecard consisted of the various groups making up the OHP membership:

1. The traditional Medicaid population (Aid to Families with Dependent Children), which includes pregnant women who have children up to age 6 and household incomes up to 133 percent of the federal poverty level; and the OHP Expansion, which includes individuals with incomes up to 100 percent of the federal poverty level

2. The Insurance Pool Governing Board, which included plans that were certified by the state to market products to employers with twenty-five or fewer employees or persons who are self-employed and have not contributed to group health insurance for the previous two years

3. The Oregon Medical Insurance Pool, which offers private health insurance to people who cannot buy conventional coverage because of preexisting medical conditions

Although all three populations were originally included in the consortium's work plan, only the Medicaid population was included in the prototype development. The unexpected difficulty of developing comparative measures resulted in the change. A key lesson learned in Oregon was that specifying a manageable target population for a scorecard is a prudent course, given the amount of effort involved in specifying, collecting, analyzing, and reporting health plan performance measures.

Unit of Comparison

Managed care health plans were specified as the unit of comparison for prototype scorecard development. In spite of the inherent difficulties in differentiating among plans, particularly when most plans have overlapping panels of physicians and hospitals, these plans were deemed the most appropriate unit for comparative purposes. The rationale for this decision was twofold: (1) health plans were the entities that consumers must choose from when selecting a health insurance option; and (2) health plans were contractually responsible and financially at-risk for the health of their members. These factors created the necessary fiscal and policy incentives for accountability at the plan level. Of equal importance, the state of Oregon had established explicit policy goals about the development of quality managed care delivery systems for OHP participants. And in the private sector, Oregon had one of the fastest-growing managed health care markets in the country.

Criteria for Indicator Selection

The consortium spent a considerable amount of time identifying, selecting, and refining the criteria that would guide the selection of indicators and information to be included on the scorecard. The five criteria adopted by consortium members were as follows:

1. *Utility by consumers.* Would the measure have utility and meaning for individual consumers?

2. *Data acquisition burden.* What would be the costs involved and the relative ease of collection?

3. *Reliability and validity.* Would the indicator be a reliable and valid measure of the process or outcome of care being measured?

4. *Educational value.* Would the indicator have some intrinsic educational value beyond representing the information preferences of individual consumers?

5. *Impact on community health.* Would the indicator also be a measure of community health improvement?

Challenges Identified

The consortium set forth a number of questions that needed to be answered, based on the following overarching policy issues identified by its members:

- What information do consumers want and need to make informed choices among health plans?
- What are the most effective formats for conveying information to consumers that would be useful in choosing a health plan?
- How do the information needs of rural consumers differ, if at all, from those of urban consumers?
- How do the information needs and preferences of persons with disabilities or chronic health conditions differ from those without such conditions?

Organizational Attributes

One methodological challenge the consortium identified early in its deliberations was how to quantify those elements of managed care organizations that vary and are of particular interest to consumers. That is, how can structural and management attributes of a health plan be specified so that the variation across plans can be elucidated and reported in a way that has utility to consumers?

Market Area Site Selection

Specifying the market for scorecard materials must take account of the insurance products to be included, as well as existing market conditions. For example, the amount of choice consumers had among health plans and how this might influence their information preferences were important considerations. In Oregon, as elsewhere, there was wide variation in choice options, depending on location but most notably in rural areas. This market dynamic needed to be factored into the overall approach to reporting and disseminating health plan information.

A major policy decision was that for both the 1996 OHP Consumer Satisfaction Survey and the pilot-testing of prototype scorecard materials, only those counties in which at least two health plans were marketed to OHP-Medicaid participants would be included. Through the development of a "managed care penetra-tion" taxonomy at the county level, where *number of health plans* became a proxy for *level of competition*, the consortium was able to identify both a *competition* and a *rural* factor for future analytical purposes. See Chapter Six for a discussion of the rural analysis plan.

Methods

The consortium's work plan included a number of activities related to synthesizing existing knowledge, collecting and analyzing pri-mary and secondary data through a focus group and committee consensus process, selecting the indicators to be included on the prototype scorecard, and nurturing the involvement of the partners to ensure ownership and buy-in for the products developed.

Information Review and Synthesis

An information review and synthesis of the extant literature in the field was completed to inform the four policy questions noted ear-lier. (Also, see Chapter Three.)

Secondary Data Analysis

Analysis of Oregon-specific morbidity and mortality data was com-pleted to determine the most prevalent health conditions of the Oregon population for information-tailoring purposes.

Two Rounds of Focus Groups. The objective of the first round of focus groups was to probe for the specific information needs and preferences of consumers when they choose a health plan. The content areas included the following:

- How consumers go about the process of selecting a health plan, including how they evaluate their options
- How consumers define quality of health care

- What the most important plan features are to present to con-sumers to assist in selecting a health plan

In the second round, we pilot-tested methods of displaying and summarizing comparative health plan performance indicators, based on the information we had gleaned from the first round of focus groups. A prototype scorecard was presented to focus group participants for their use, and it was critiqued during the sessions. (For a comprehensive discussion of the focus group methods and findings, see Chapter Four.)

Pilot-Testing Health Plan Performance Measures. Through an analysis of the data specifications currently used by health plans, including assessing their comparability across health plans, the consortium pilot-tested the collection and reporting of three Med-icaid HEDIS measures. (See Chapter Seven for a discussion of this activity.)

Nurturing Stakeholder Involvement

Among the most critical activities of the consortium was that of nurturing and facilitating the continuing involvement of all affected stakeholders. As is often the case in such partnerships, the lay public (consumers) have the most difficult time making their voices heard. The consortium effort was no exception. Keeping consumers at the table became increasingly difficult during the move from the information-gathering stage to the knowledge-building and pilot-testing phases. The paternalism that the author warns about in Chapter One became a pronounced influence as scorecard designers attempted to balance the expressed information needs and preferences of consumers with the art of the possible in terms of measurement and reporting.

The rest of this book describes the unique learning and knowl-edge-building experience of the state of Oregon and its citizens. In spite of the many fine academic projects related to scorecard development that have been completed around the country, or those currently in process, the Oregon Consumer Scorecard Consortium represents a unique statewide, broadly participatory experience. This experience was a noteworthy effort, particularly the challenges and opportunities encountered in pursuing both the science and art of measuring and reporting health care quality in the context of a dynamic and heterogeneous human laboratory.

Chapter Three

Consumer Preferences

Issues of Perception and Measurement

Pamela P. Hanes and Holly B. Jimison

The Oregon consortium drew heavily on the experiences and wisdom of others in shaping its prototype scorecard. Information from other projects around the country and from the health services research and communications literature informed the design of two rounds of focus groups held in the fall of 1995 and spring of 1996.

The literature on consumers' need for health insurance information has grown in proportion to the increase in numbers of managed care, health-insuring organizations. As discussed in Chapter One, a great reliance has been placed on competitive markets to improve quality and value in health services delivery. This emphasis has spawned an industry that produces consumer information material.

Oregon's interest in producing consumer information was fueled by the state's policy objective of ensuring that consumers had sufficient information to make informed choices in their health plan selection. Early research questions surfaced related to the legislative mandate to address individual consumers' health plan information needs through a consumer scorecard. The questions were as follows:

- What health insurance information is meaningful and useful to consumers for choice purposes?
- What plan features and performance measures should be included on a consumer-oriented scorecard?

- How much information should be included on a consumer scorecard?
- What is the appropriate unit (or units) of analysis for comparative health plan information reporting—health insurance organizations? clinics? hospitals? physicians and other health care professionals?

Consumer Knowledge

We undertook a review and synthesis of the literature in the field during the spring of 1995. Not much literature was available that illuminated the factors affecting consumers' knowledge of health insurance and the effects of that knowledge on health plan choice. Most studies had not looked specifically at managed care, although some could be generalized to consumers in a managed care environment.

Marquis (1983) found that the majority of consumers understood the characteristics of their health insurance when the benefits were simple; education, race, and income were associated with level of understanding. Others found that consumers did not have adequate knowledge or information to make informed decisions about more complex types of coverage.

Several studies showed that older consumers were relatively uneducated about Medicare coverage and uncertain as to which services were provided under Medicare without co-payments (Davidson, 1988; McCall, Rice, and Sangl, 1986; Rice, 1987). McCall found that consumers with higher education and incomes consistently knew more about Medicare coverage but that older people generally know little about basic coverage and benefits. As a result, Medicare beneficiaries found it difficult to make informed decisions about purchasing Medicare supplemental coverage (McCall, Rice, and Sangl, 1986).

Garnick and her colleagues (1993) reviewed consumers' understanding of their health insurance coverage and postulated six factors that account for the general lack of consumer knowledge they found. These are as follows:

1. Health plans do not communicate information in ways that enrollees can easily understand and assimilate.
2. People tend to be interested in coverage details only when they are ill and in need of care.
3. People covered by multiple health plans are confused about the coordination of benefits.
4. Knowledge of coverage is associated with recent experience with a health plan, higher income, and higher levels of education.
5. People tend not to know about services or benefits they do not anticipate using.
6. For some benefits, coverage is so minimal that many beneficiaries perceive the service not to be covered.

Consumer Interest in Health Plan Information

A study investigating the factors associated with consumer interest in health plan information found that female heads of households were most likely to use comparative information to choose coverage for their families (Klinkman, 1991). Among the elderly, Davidson found that higher levels of interest in comparative health insurance information was associated with being female and white, having higher income, being in the early stages of chronic disease, and lacking a regular source of health care (Davidson, 1988).

McGee and Hunter (1992) found that consumers planning a change in health care coverage were most interested in comparative plan information that highlighted significant plan differences. Additionally, she found that when consumers heard negative assessments from other consumers about the integrity of plan survey data, they would not use it to make choices.

Using different criteria, Juba, Lave, and Shaddy (1990) found additional factors that were related to consumers' interest in comparative plan information. These included poverty, attitudes about risk, lack of an established physician relationship, and positive attitudes about innovation and change. Both Mechanic (1989) and Pemberton (1990) found that benefit and coverage information were not important to most people until they became sick.

Consumer Choice of Health Plans

Several investigators have studied consumer purchasing decisions to better understand individual preferences and needs for information. Mechanic (1989) observed that individuals will narrow choices to a psychologically manageable set, focusing primarily on indicators of satisfaction, access, and physicians' interest and responsiveness to their concerns. This was particularly true when consumers were faced with a number of choices.

When faced with complexity, consumers are more likely to rely on their personal preferences. Mechanic (1989) observed that these preferences were largely influenced by an individual's location in the life cycle and in family status, by psychological factors related to uncertainty, by the time required to acquire new information, and by the limits of understanding how various plans function. He further noted that consumers try to make rational decisions but are often thwarted because information is difficult to obtain, plans vary widely in their benefit structure, and cost sharing, as well as the literature describing plan features, are confusing. The features of health plans found to be particularly salient in consumer choice were an existing patient-physician relationship, ability of the plan to meet special care needs, and cost.

Cost was found to be the most common feature of importance to consumers in several studies examining decisions about health insurance choice. The ability to retain one's physician was also found to be highly salient in several studies (Berki, Penchansky, Fortus, and Ashcraft, 1978; Juba, Lave, and Shaddy, 1990; McGee and Hunter, 1992; Scitovsky, McCall, and Benham, 1978; Scotti, Bonner, and Wiman, 1986; Sofaer, 1993).

Weaver found that consumers' perceptions of technical skills were an important factor in assessing the desirability of hospitals affiliated with health plans and subsequent health plan choice (Weaver, 1989). Similarly, assessing the competency of physicians affiliated with health plans, perceived communication skills, caring attitudes, access to high technology, and reputation, were all considered important factors in choosing a plan (Jensen, Marino, and Clough, 1992).

At the health plan level, ease of access to services, reported satisfaction of family and friends, and comprehensiveness of benefits, were all found to be informational domains of interest to consumers (Berki, Penchansky, Fortus, and Ashcraft, 1978; Hiramatsu, 1990; Juba and Lave, and Shaddy, 1990; Klinkman, 1991; McGee and Hunter, 1992; Rubin and others, 1993; Scitovsky, McCall, and Benham, 1978; Scotti, Bonner, and Wiman, 1986; Weaver, 1989).

Several studies have found that consumers report facing significant challenges in choosing a health plan. Both Mechanic and Sofaer report that consumers tend not to seek out health coverage information because of its relatively high "search costs" (Mechanic, 1989; Sofaer, 1993). Davidson (1988) and Rice (1987) found that consumers were unable to make informed choices because the wide variation in benefits and coverage is confusing. Specifically, the materials provided to consumers were too abstract and contained terms that were difficult to understand, thereby thwarting consumers' best efforts at making an informed choice. Davidson also found that older consumers frequently experienced difficulty processing large amounts of complex information.

Likewise, Schuttinga, Falik, and Steinwaol (1985) report that Medicare beneficiaries find it difficult to make informed choices using benefit information. Davidson, Sofaer, and Gertler (1992) report that choice about supplemental Medicare insurance is influenced by the interaction between amount of insurance information and health status. Sofaer, Kenney, and Davidson (1992) used an innovative illness episode approach (IEA) to assess Medicare consumers' health insurance choices by making information more relevant to their own health care experience. The IEA provided descriptions to Medicare beneficiaries of the consequences of different choices based on specific illness examples.

Using a pretest-posttest design, these investigators found that IEA workshop participants reduced their out-of-pocket health care expenditures and were more satisfied with the changes made in coverage than a control group that didn't receive the information. In a later study, IEA workshop participants were more likely to drop duplicate coverage, spend less on premiums, and be satisfied with their decision to change coverage. However, the research team found that workshop participants' overall insurance knowledge was not any greater than that of the control group.

Decision-Making Models

Relatively few studies have focused on how consumers use plan and provider information to make health care choices. *Descriptive models* of consumer choice suggest that consumers will weigh their health risks and their expected costs and benefits under competing choice options. These models describe how consumers compare the options available to them. But the *subjective expected utility model* provides one theoretical construct for how decision makers evaluate their risks, costs, and benefits. It also provides a theoretical framework for how decision makers make trade-offs among desirable and undesirable features of health plan options (Raiffa, 1968).

Chakraborty, Ettenson, and Gaeth (1994) found that consumer choice was affected by as many as nineteen health plan attributes and that the importance of these attributes varied across different demographic groups. The most important attribute for consumer choice was hospitalization coverage, followed by choice of doctor, amount of premium, dental coverage, and choice of hospital.

Consumer Surveys

Investigators have relied heavily on satisfaction surveys to infer consumers' information needs and preferences. The survey items most strongly associated with consumer choice are those that assess the patient-provider interaction. Physician attributes most often associated with satisfied patients include effective communications, responsiveness to patients' requests, availability for after-hours care, personal caring attitude, perceived technical skill, allowing sufficient time for an office visit, and courteousness (Cleary and McNeil, 1988; Crane and Lynch, 1988; DiMatteo, Prince, and Taranta, 1979; Hiramatsu, 1990; Lim and Zallocco, 1988; Murphy-Cullen and Larsen, 1984).

In addition, researchers have found that perceived adequacy of health facilities and equipment, access and convenience of clinics, and length of time as a health plan member were all associated with higher levels of patient satisfaction (Cleary and McNeil, 1988; Gray, 1980; Hiramatsu, 1990; Ware, Davies-Avery, and Stewart, 1978). Even when the hospital was the target of the satisfaction survey, the most highly correlated item with satisfaction was the provider-patient interaction, for example, how well patients' concerns were met and how satisfied they were with nursing care (Abramowitz, Cote, and Berry, 1987).

Others have surveyed consumers directly to determine what information would be useful in choosing a health plan. Hibbard and Jewett (1994) used both written surveys and focus groups to study consumers' comprehension of HEDIS measures. Their findings suggest that only a subset of indicators currently being included on report cards are considered useful by consumers. Foremost among these were patients' self-reported ratings of quality and satisfaction. Indicators judged to be less useful were certain condition-specific health plan performance measures (for example, childhood immunizations) that were not relevant to the respondents' current or expected health care experience.

Gold and Woodridge (1994) reviewed the current state of health-plan-sponsored surveys in terms of focus, instrumentation, and survey methods. These authors found that the *content* was better developed than the methods used for administering satisfaction surveys. Three recommendations developed from their instrument critique were (1) to increase public availability of survey tools and provide construct documentation, (2) to support more research on methodological issues such as developing methods for risk-adjusting survey results, and (3) to develop more effective, user-friendly consumer information materials.

Sherbourne, Hays, and Burton (1994) reported that items used to measure access and satisfaction had not been adequately tested for internal validity or reliability. They suggested that this methodological rigor ought to be applied to survey items before they are included on national surveys and that indicators be standardized across survey instruments. The recommendations of Gold, Woodridge, and Sherbourne have been included in the work plan of the Consumer Assessment of Health Plans Survey (CAHPS) project, a multiyear study currently being sponsored by the federal Agency for Health Care Policy and Research (AHCPR).

Cronin (1994) studied how group purchasers use consumer surveys and quality information in their decision making about which plans to offer their employees. The purchasers studied included Xerox, Digital, Tenneco, California Public Employees Retirement System, Cleveland Health Quality Choice, and General Telephone and Electric studies have found that only a handful of employers provide consumer satisfaction ratings and health plan performance information to their employees (General Accounting Office, 1994; Hoy, Wicks, and Forland, 1996). Likewise, a national survey recently conducted for the Kaiser Family Foundation and AHCPR found that only 39 percent of all Americans reported having seen any information comparing the quality of health plans, doctors, or hospitals within the year prior to being surveyed (Kaiser Family Foundation, 1996).

Focus Groups

Several teams of researchers have conducted focus groups to investigate what information consumers find helpful in choosing among health plans (Benova, 1995; Frederick/Schneiders, 1995; McGee, Sofaer, and Kreling, 1996). Kaiser Family Foundation, NCQA, and AHCPR each sponsored a series of focus groups addressing a variety of issues, including how consumers define quality, how consumers identify features of health plans that are important to them, how consumers make decisions among health plans, and what sources of information consumers use in choosing a health plan. The focus groups also included hands-on evaluation of the content and format of a number of scorecard models.

Similar results were observed across each set of focus groups. In general, participants were interested in hearing about the experiences of other consumers like themselves. Topics of primary concern included whether

- Services were readily accessible.
- Providers appeared to care about patients.
- They were able to see their own doctor or choose a doctor who made them feel comfortable.
- There were administrative hassles with the plan.
- Plan information was presented clearly and was relevant to the issues they were dealing with at the time.

Few consistent patterns emerged in terms of preferred content and format for a scorecard. The NCQA focus groups heard similar responses to what information consumers most wanted:

- Costs for expected health care utilization
- How the health plan works
- Scope of physician choice

- Consumer satisfaction ratings regarding accessibility and physician quality
- Unbiased expert judgment about quality
- Only information that is relevant to them as individuals

Findings from focus groups conducted in the Portland metropolitan area by Benova, Inc., identified specific criteria that consumers use in selecting a health plan, including access to primary care doctors and specialists, clinic locations, past experience with a health plan, and access to all types of care, facilities, and equipment.

Between January and March of 1995, the Kaiser Family Foundation funded fourteen focus groups of Medicare beneficiaries to talk about managed care. Focus group participants were representative of one of three groups: (1) Medicare beneficiaries in managed care, primarily HMOs; (2) Medicare beneficiaries with traditional fee-for-service coverage; and (3) consumers from sixty to sixty-five years old who were about to become Medicare beneficiaries. The findings from these discussions included the following:

- Word of mouth played an important role in choosing an HMO.
- Participants felt heavily recruited as they approached Medicare eligibility.
- Participants varied in how they preferred to receive information; many expressed a preference for printed brochures, while others preferred to talk one-on-one with an HMO representative, attend meetings, presentations, or have telephone interviews.
- Participants expressed concern about the objectivity of brochures and sales presentations conducted by insuring organizations.

The information that participants found to be most useful in choosing a health plan included the following: how to access one's own doctor; the costs associated with premiums, co-payments, and supplemental insurance; the availability of additional benefits such as prescription drugs; whether there was a single entry point for appointments and referrals; satisfaction ratings of individuals like oneself; and whether physicians in available health plans were properly screened and credentialed.

Researchers in these various projects found that consumers give greater importance to patient satisfaction ratings than they do to clinical process and outcome indicators of health care quality. For example, when presented with population-based performance measures such as pediatric asthma hospitalizations, mammography, and immunization rates, consumers were either uncertain as to what dimension of quality was being measured, or they noted that the measure was more an indicator of individual health behavior than health plan performance (Hibbard and Jewett, 1994). A subsequent report from the same investigators concluded that these technical quality measures were not as important to consumers because they lacked a basic understanding of managed care and therefore did not have a context for evaluating the measure (Hibbard and Jewett, 1997).

Since our review and synthesis of the literature in 1995, Gibbs, Sangl, and Burrus held a series of twenty-two focus groups in eight locations around the country to probe for consumer needs for health plan choice information. Their findings add to the growing body of evidence that consumers "lack[ed] the information needed to assess their rights as consumers or the health plan's justifiable limits on services and providers," further, "that increasing consumers' awareness of what they should expect from plans and how they should proceed if their rights are not respected would empower consumers to deal more effectively with their current plan, and over time, influence the health care environment as they seek out more responsive plans" (Gibbs, Sangl, and Burrus, 1996, p. 72).

From Literature Review to Work Plan

In general, the research on consumers' preferences for choice information had involved employed, privately insured individuals and, to a lesser extent, Medicare beneficiaries. The dearth of research on Medicaid enrollees left a number of unanswered questions that the Oregon Consumer Scorecard Consortium needed to address. These unanswered questions helped to shape the conceptual framework and project work plan of the consortium.

References

Abramowitz, S., Cote, A. A., and Berry, E. "Analyzing Patient Satisfaction: A Multianalytic Approach." *Quality Review Bulletin,* 1987, *13*(4), 122–130.

Benova, Inc. *Choice Card: A Medicaid/Medicare Consumers Values/Preferences and Report Card Model for Health Plan Selection.* Report to Agency for Health Care Policy and Research, Contract No. 282–94–2031, 1995.

Berki, S. E., Penchansky, R., Fortus, R. S., and Ashcraft, M. L. "Enrollment Choices in Different Types of HMO's: A Multivariate Analysis. *Medical Care,* 1978, *16*(8), 682–697.

Chakraborty, G., Ettenson, R., and Gaeth, G. "How Consumers Choose Health Insurance." *Journal of Health Care Market,* 1994, *14*(1), 21–33.

Cleary, P., and McNeil, B. "Patient Satisfaction as an Indicator of Quality of Care." *Inquiry,* 1988, *25,* 25–36.

Crane, F. G., and Lynch, J. E. "Consumer Selection of Physicians and Dentists: An Examination of Choice Criteria and Cue Usage." *Journal of Health Care Marketing,* 1988, 8(3), 4–15.

Cronin, C. *Using Health Care Quality Information: Employer Case Studies.* Draft report prepared for the Agency for Health Care Policy and Research, Contract No. 282–91–0027, 1994.

Davidson, B. N. "Designing Health Insurance Information for the Medicare Beneficiary: A Policy Synthesis." *Health Services Research,* 1988, *23*(5), 685–719.

Davidson, B. N., Sofaer, S., and Gertler, P. "Consumer Information and Biased Selection in the Demand for Coverage Supplementing Medicare. *Social Science Medicine,* 1992, *34*(9), 1023–1034.

DiMatteo, M. R., Prince, L. M., and Taranta, A. "Patients' Perceptions of Physicians' Behavior: Determinants of Patient Commitment to the Therapeutic Relationship." *Journal of Community Health,* 1979, 4(4), 280–290.

Frederick/Schneiders, Inc. "Analysis of Focus Groups Concerning Managed Care and Medicare." Report prepared for the Henry J. Kaiser Family Foundation, Washington, D.C., 1995.

Garnick, D., Hendricks, A., Thorpe, K., Newhouse, J., Danelan, K., and Blendon, R. "How Well Do Americans Understand Their Health Care Coverage?" *Health Affairs,* 1993, *12*(3), 204–212.

General Accounting Office. "Report Cards Are Useful, but Significant Issues Need to Be Addressed." *Health Education and Human Services Division*, HEHS-94-219, 1994.

Gibbs, D. A., Sangl, J. A., and Burrus, B. "Consumer Perspectives on Information Needs for Health Plan Choice." *Health Care Financing Review*, 1996, *18*(1), 55–73.

Gold, M., and Woodridge, J. "Plan-Based Surveys of Satisfaction with Access and Quality of Care: Review and Critique." Draft report prepared for Agency for Health Care Policy and Research under subcontract to Health Systems Research, Inc., Contract No. 282-91-0027, 1994.

Gray, L. C. "Consumer Satisfaction with Physician Provider Services: A Panel Study." *Social Science and Medicine*, 1980, *14*(A), 65–75.

Hibbard, J. H., and Jewett, J. J. "Preliminary Findings from Consumer Comprehension of Quality Care Indicators." Report to Agency for Health Care Policy and Research, R01-08231, 1994.

Hibbard J. H., and Jewett J. J. "Will Quality Report Cards Help Consumers?" *Health Affairs*, 1997, *16*(3), 218–228.

Hiramatsu, S. "Member Satisfaction in a Staff-Model Health Maintenance Organization." *American Journal Hospital Pharmacy*, 1990, *47*(10), 2270–2273.

Hoy, E. W., Wicks, E. K., and Forland, R. A. "A Guide to Facilitating Consumer Choice." *Health Affairs*, 1996, *15*(4), 9–30.

Jensen, D. K., Marino, P. B., and Clough, J. D. "A Consumer's Guide for Marketing Medical Services: One Institution's Experience." *Quarterly Quality Review Bulletin*, 1992, *18*, 164–171.

Juba, D. A., Lave, J. R., and Shaddy, J. "An Analysis of the Choice of Health Benefits Plans." *Inquiry*, 1990, *17*(1), 62–71.

Kaiser Family Foundation and Agency for Health Care Policy and Research. "Americans as Health Care Consumers: The Role of Quality Information." Survey conducted by Princeton Survey Research Associates, Oct. 1996.

Klinkman, M. S. "The Process of Choice of Health Care Plan and Provider: Development of an Integrated Analytic Framework." *Medical Care Review*, 1991, *48*(3), 295–330.

Lim, J. S., and Zallocco, R. "Determinant Attributes in Formulation of Attitudes Toward Four Health Care Systems." *Journal of Health Care Marketing*, 1988, 8(2), 25–30.

Marquis, M. S. "Consumers' Knowledge About Their Health Insurance Coverage." *Health Care Financing Review*, 1983, *5*(1), 65–79.

McCall, N., Rice, T., and Sangl, J. "Consumer Knowledge of Medicare and Supplemental Health Insurance Benefits." *Health Services Research*, 1986, *20*(6), 633–657.

McGee, J., and Hunter, M. "Employee Response to Health Benefits Survey Results Brochure: Findings from Fall 1992 Interviews." Final report to State of Minnesota Department of Employee Relations, Dec. 1992.

48 Grading Health Care

McGee, J., Sofaer, S., and Kreling, B. "Medicare and Medicaid Consumer Information Projects Findings from Focus Groups." Report prepared for the National Committee on Quality Assurance, 1996.

Mechanic, D. "Consumer Choice Among Health Insurance Options." *Health Affairs*, 1989, 8(1), 18–48.

Murphy-Cullen, C. L., and Larsen, L. C. "Interaction Between the Socio-Demographic Variables of Physicians and Their Patients: Its Impact on Patient Satisfaction." *Social Science and Medicine*, 1984, 19(2), 163–166.

Pemberton, J. H. "The Elderly Consumer: A Critical Review of Information Source Use and Advertising Recommendations." *Health Services Management Research*, 1990, 3(2), 127–136.

Raiffa, H. *Decision Analysis: Introductory Lectures on Choices Under Uncertainty.* Menlo Park, Calif.: Addison-Wesley, 1968.

Rice, T. "Economic Assessment of Health Care for the Elderly." *Milbank Memorial Fund Quarterly*, 1987, 65(4), 488–520.

Rubin, H. R., Gandek, B., Rogers, W. H., Kosinski, M., McHorney, C. A., and Ware, J. E. "Patients' Ratings of Outpatient Visit in Different Practice Settings: Results from the Medical Outcomes Study." *Journal of the American Medical Association*, 1993, 270, 835–840.

Schuttinga, J. A., Falik, M., and Steinwaol, B. "Health Plan Selection in the Federal Employees' Health Benefits Program." *Journal of Health Politics, Policy and Law*, 1985, 10(1), 119–139.

Scitovsky, A., McCall, N., and Benham, L. "Factors Affecting the Choice Between Two Prepaid Plans." *Medical Care*, 1978, 16(8), 57–69.

Scotti, D. J., Bonner, P. G., and Wiman, A. R. "An Analysis of the Determinants of HMO Reenrollment Behavior: Implications for Theory and Policy." *Journal of Health Care Marketing*, 1986, 6(2), 7–16.

Sherbourne, C., Hays, R., and Burton, T. "Population-Based Surveys of Access and Patient Satisfaction." Draft report prepared for the Agency for Health Care Policy Research, subcontracted to Health Systems Research, Contract No. 282–91–6027. RAND Corporation, 1994.

Sofaer, S. "Informing and Protecting Consumers Under Managed Competition." *Health Affairs*, 1993 (Supplement), pp. 76–86.

Sofaer, S., Kenney, E., and Davidson, B. "The Effect of the Illness Episode Approach on Medicare Beneficiaries' Health Insurance Decisions." *Health Services Research*, 1992, 27(5), 671–693.

Ware, J. E., Davies-Avery, A., and Stewart, A. L. "The Measurement and Meaning of Patient Satisfaction." *Health and Medical Care Services Review*, 1978, 1(1), 3–15.

Weaver, F. J. "Quality Indicators for the Market Perspective." *Topics in Health Records: Management*, 1989, 10(2), 73–76.

Chapter Four

Consumers Want Choice and Voice

Michael J. Garland, Barry F. Anderson,
and H. Diana Jones

Health plan scorecards can aid consumers in two important ways. They can (1) provide information to consumers about how competing health plans differ (choice) and (2) provide information to health plans about consumers' assessments of service, access, and quality (voice). This dual function has the potential to improve both the quality and value of health care services being delivered through a new generation of health-insuring organizations.

In this chapter, we report on the recommendations for scorecard content and design made by Oregon consumers during two rounds of focus groups. Drawing on the experiences of people previously not included in scorecard-related focus group research, the Oregon Consumer Scorecard Project recruited individuals with chronic health conditions and significant disabilities and those living in rural areas of the state. Focus groups included adults between the ages of eighteen and sixty-four years who were enrolled in the Oregon Health Plan (OHP) Medicaid program, as well as individuals covered by private, employer-based health insurance. The target populations were persons with significant chronic conditions and disabilities and persons living in rural areas of the state.

The published literature about consumers' perceptions of health care quality and their knowledge of health insurance options was limited. Also limited was information about how consumers' knowledge about options affects their information preferences and how health plan information facilitates decision making.

Oregon Scorecard Focus Groups

Oregon Health Decisions, a civic organization dedicated to promoting citizen participation in health policy issues, conducted the focus groups under contract with the Oregon Health Policy Institute. Based on project staff's review and synthesis of earlier focus group research, we expected that consumers would identify cost, personal physician availability, and benefits and coverage as critical information to be included in health plan choice materials. It was also apparent that consumers would have widely varying information needs and preferences, depending on where they lived and how healthy they were.

Focus groups can be a powerful learning tool. For the consortium, they provided an opportunity to find out what information consumers found useful in selecting among competing health plans and how that information could be used to provide feedback to plans concerning quality, access, and value. This voice would come from people who were not technical experts but were consumers of health care goods and services.

Because a consumer-oriented scorecard would involve adapting instruments previously developed and used by experts, we thought it was important to set aside preconceptions about what information consumers *should* use to make rational decisions. Instead, in the first round of focus groups we asked the question, What information would you find useful for making a choice among health plans? We started with a clean slate, as opposed to providing participants with examples of existing scorecards and asking them to comment on their usefulness. We had learned from previous focus groups that existing performance measures (for example, HEDIS) should be used as discussion probes only, after first allowing participants to establish their own frame of reference for the measure. Starting with a clean slate avoids prematurely narrowing informational options while still allowing group facilitators to probe for the potential relevance of expert constructions of health care quality.

When insight into consumers' information preferences was clearer, the next step in the scorecard development process was to display this information in alternate formats, probing for what constituted the most useful ways of presenting the desired information. The basic research plan, therefore, was to hold two rounds of focus group sessions, first asking what information consumers wanted, then asking how the desired information might be presented most usefully.

Strengths and Limitations of Focus Group Research

Primary among the merits of focus group research is its capacity to structure a problem from the user's perspective (Krueger, 1988). Focus groups can create an environment in which participants engage in organized discussions that stimulate thought and thus produce a synergistic effect. If sessions are well facilitated, participants will evoke in one another ideas and dimensions of a specific range of topics by stating personal opinions while listening to those expressed by others. Even when participants disagree, the articulation of differences can clarify and establish relevance, and thereby serve to distill and illuminate the most salient information.

The Oregon focus groups were an effective method for producing a checklist that scorecard designers could then use to incorporate issues important to consumers into a final scorecard product. A checklist serves designers by helping them systematically recall important information that might otherwise be overlooked. Using the checklist developed in round one, scorecard designers had a practical tool for incorporating content identified by consumers, as well as an accounting tool for tracking decisions about whether or not to include specific items in the scorecard prototype to be pilot-tested in the second round.

Because focus group participation was limited to between ten and fifteen members per group, and because participants were not sampled randomly, it would have been inappropriate to assign weights or otherwise attempt to quantify the information gleaned from these discussions. Quantitative research methods can be used as a follow-up to focus group findings once domains of interest have been identified. For example, large, random-sample surveys may be developed to establish the relative value of information domains. In the absence of a link to quantitative methods, final judgments about the relative importance of various items must be left to the decision makers.

Round One: Information Consumers Want

In the first round of Oregon focus groups (fall of 1995), participants were asked to identify *categories* of information that they would find useful for selecting a health plan. In designing the format for the first round, consortium members specified two policy areas to be pursued:

1. What categories of information do individual consumers identify as relevant in making a choice among available health plans? Does this information vary by health status, particularly among persons with disabilities and chronic health conditions?

2. Does geography influence the information needs of consumers, particularly for those who live in rural areas? Does the fact of living in a rural area alter the range of concerns expressed?

Focus group participants shared responsibility for summarizing the key findings from each meeting. Working together, they described what kinds of information would be useful on a hypothetical scorecard designed to help them choose a health plan. The end product of the first round of focus groups was a checklist of ideas from participants. This checklist identified what categories of information consumers found most relevant for choice decision-making purposes (see Exhibit 4.1).

Exhibit 4.1. The Design Checklist.

Broad Categories	Content Issue	Included Page #	Not used because . . .
Hot Button Issues	How can enrollees find out about which plan their current physician participates in?		
	How can enrollees find out about which plan is most successful in helping members get access to dental care?		
General Organizational Features of the Plans	How can enrollees find out about which local providers participate in which plan and are taking new patients?		
	How do plans help enrollees with: • Finding providers? • Referrals? • Appealing decisions?		
	How do the plans assist with with coordinating payments among Medicaid, Medicare, and billing enrollees for direct payments?		
Specific Services	How do plans differ in terms of access to regular, urgent, and emergency care?		
	Approach to preventive programs?		
	Access to addiction recovery and smoking cessation programs?		
	Health education programs?		
	Coordination of care for persons with chronic conditions and special care needs (e.g., specialist care, home care, long-term care)?		

Exhibit 4.1. The Design Checklist, continued.

Broad Categories	Content Issue	Included Page #	Not used because . . .
Specific Services, *continued*	Access to nonmedical health services?		
	How do plans handle appeals regarding uncovered services?		
	Social support services related to health care (e.g., transportation, respite care, child care)?		
	How do plans differ in contracts with local pharmacies and distributors of supplies and equipment?		
	Do the plans differ in the way they authorize care received out of their service area?		
Quality of Care Issues	How do plans differ on the technical quality of care delivered by their participating providers? • HEDIS measures (specify)		
	How do plans differ in the way patients and enrollees evaluate them? • Medicaid enrollees? • People with special health care needs? • Minorities? • People from local rural area?		
	How do plans differ in how they seek and respond to feedback from enrollees? • Feedback to providers? • Feedback about administrative efficiency issues?		
	Do the plans differ in their efforts to promote respectful care and protect members from discrimination?		

As it turned out, the ideas consumers brought up were driven both by choice factors and by the desire to give feedback to health plans about individual concerns and overall satisfaction with the care and services received. The general topics discussed were grouped into the following categories:

In which plan is my physician? For those who were eligible for Medicaid and those who were privately insured as well, there was a first-order concern about knowing physicians' plan affiliations. For individuals who had an existing relationship with a physician, knowing which plan or plans the physician was affiliated with was of prime importance.

What is the level of cost sharing? This factor was of concern to individuals with employer-based private insurance. For these focus group participants, premium contributions varied by product offered and included both deductibles and co-insurance. As a result, comparative information about cost-sharing arrangements was of great interest to those who faced this consideration when choosing a health plan.

How are health plans different? Focus group participants noted that any attempt at producing a comparative scorecard should be done so that the information presented represents real, meaningful, and understandable differences from an ordinary person's perspective. Many participants complained about getting excessive information that did not illuminate real differences among health plans but rather served to create confusion and to clutter the decision-making process. Among Medicaid enrollees, because benefits and coverage were identical in available plans, these factors were superfluous to their decision-making needs. Medicaid participants were, however, keenly interested in the differences in how plans *managed care*. Benefits and coverage differences among health plans were very important to privately insured consumers.

How do we navigate through managed care organizations? Participants in both the Medicaid and privately insured focus groups expressed anxiety and concern about their lack of knowledge about managed care and what to expect from health plans in this regard. It was noted that a scorecard, or other choice tool, should help potential plan members understand the service differences among health plans and how both routine care and special health care problems are handled. Understanding that managed care organizations are complex social systems, participants reported that information describing the differences between (or among) plans in how they manage care and how they help members navigate the system would be very useful in making an informed choice. This information is most helpful to persons with chronic health problems and disabling conditions.

How do health plans take care of people like me? Focus group participants advised that a useful scorecard would provide information that was tailored to the individual needs of consumers based on social, demographic, or health status factors. Attention should be paid to lifespan factors such as the special information needs of families with young children or older adults and how these factors might influence their need for information about health plans. Again, mention was made of the unique information needs of people with chronic health problems, particularly in the areas of care management and access to specialists. Finally, a clear message was sent by rural focus group members that they were not interested in information about the performance of health plans in metropolitan areas; they wanted to know about the options available where they lived.

Will I be able to get help interpreting scorecard information? A scorecard will ultimately be useful if it is accompanied by access to a person who is trained to help answer consumers' questions, interpret their needs, and guide them to relevant health plan and provider information. Focus group participants suggested that even the most well-designed scorecard would fall short of meeting their information needs if they didn't have ready access to an informed person to assist them in working through the information presented.

Are health plans responsive to member feedback? Scorecard efforts should be a vehicle for providing member feedback to health plans about their satisfaction with the quality of health plan performance. Consumers spontaneously brought up this dimension of scorecard use, although the meeting materials focused only on the task of choosing among competing health plans.

Round Two: Displaying Health Plan Information

In the second round of focus groups (spring of 1996), participants were asked to use and critique a prototype, paper-based scorecard developed using information obtained during round one. Along with the paper-based guide, alternative formats of presentation (telephone, video, and computers) were introduced to foster discussion about how information can best be presented to maximize its usefulness and effectiveness.

Several sources of information guided the selection of indicators for the prototype scorecard pilot-tested in round two. These sources included findings from the first round of focus groups, input from the consortium's consumer committee, the health plans' assessment of their data collection capabilities, and the knowledge gleaned from the literature review and synthesis, supplemented by knowledge from the field of communications research.

The findings from the first round of focus groups were thus shaped into a set of stimulus materials for the second round of sessions. The second-round participants were given an actual scorecard and asked to work through it as though they were about to select a health plan. They then were asked to critique its usefulness and understandability in a group discussion.

The primary stimulus used was a paper-based prototype scorecard titled "A Consumer Guide to Selecting a Health Plan" (see Appendix A). This twenty-two–page prototype scorecard incorporated comparative data from Oregon health plans; the data were identified by fictitious names. The decision to blind the health plans' identity was driven by a desire to elicit reactions to how the information was presented rather than trigger debates about the merits of particular plans. At the same time, this gave us a chance to present real data, to the extent possible, that captured the attributes of Oregon's plans.

Prototype Scorecard Features

The basic scorecard prototype contained five sections: (1) common benefits and services; (2) provider information on physician and hospital plan affiliations; (3) member satisfaction ratings; (4) health plan performance data relating to processes of care; and (5) integrated information relating to a specific health topic (maternity care).

The materials given to participants at the beginning of the focus group included a copy of the Consumer Guide and a worksheet on which they could keep track of their choice criterion priorities as they moved through the booklet. In addition to the paper-based scorecard, alternative media were presented during the session for participants' critique (computers, video, and an 800–number telephone line).

As with the challenges encountered in collecting valid and reliable data (see Chapters Six and Seven), the consortium staff was challenged with finding ways to present the broad range of information reported as important to consumers in a sufficient level of detail to be personally relevant while not overwhelming scorecard users with unnecessarily detailed information.

In response to the strong recommendation for descriptive information about managed care that was voiced during the first round of focus groups, we had the opportunity in the prototype materials to describe the standard managed care benefit package offered to OHP-Medicaid enrollees. The uniformity of this information allowed the group facilitators to probe for the degree of comprehension achieved in the terms and phrases selected to describe managed care, benefits, and coverage levels. In developing these prototype materials, we drew from informational materials developed by Benova, Inc. (1995) for the Health Care Financing Administration (HCFA) to describe the basic elements of managed care to Medicare and Medicaid populations.

Service and Organizational Attributes

In recognition of the organizational and management differences among plans, we included examples of service features where plans differed in order to probe for the utility of this information to consumers making choices. Service features mentioned repeatedly in focus groups included the processes used for getting referred to a specialist, requirements for service pre-authorization, grievances procedures, and access to advice and care after office hours.

Specifying and displaying this descriptive information in a comparative format was not without its challenges. The gulf between what an organization says it provides to its customers and what consumers experience is often wide. This was best illustrated in the differences noted by consumers in the marketing materials they had received from health plans describing coverage and benefits and how consumers reported their experiences of a service as actually delivered.

Working with the health plan members participating in the consortium, a survey was conducted to gather objective information on a range of topics of high interest to consumers (see "Request for Descriptive Navigational Information" in Appendix B). The survey included questions about accessing care, referral processes, quality assurance programs, grievance procedures, and unique features of maternity care services. Translating the plan responses to this survey into useable information for the scorecard was difficult. It involved discerning the components of the service, ferreting out real differences among plans, and displaying this comparative information in an objective, precise, and useable format.

This exercise demonstrated one of the major challenges to scorecard development; that is, translating service elements that are of
great interest to consumers into comparative, marketing-neutral,
information "sound bites" for comparative reporting purposes.

Provider Access

Displaying physician- and hospital-level information on a scorecard will be a monumental undertaking. We learned from Oregon
consumers what the state's Medicaid agency had known for some
time as a result of its 800–number hotline. Although physician
availability by health plan is highly important to consumers, that
information is elusive. Physicians open and close their practices so
frequently that accurate, up-to-date information about physician
status cannot be gathered economically.

Although that problem is still unresolved, the scorecard prototype included a hypothetical 800–number to test consumer reac-
tion to this scorecard feature. As anticipated, it was well received
among focus group participants. In a similar fashion, the scorecard
included a map of hospital locations for the area in which focus
groups were held to test whether this information display would be
useful to consumers in making choices. Hospital location was
equally well received, and the good news is that existing mapping
capabilities make this geographically sensitive information easily
accessible for inclusion on a scorecard.

Consumer Satisfaction Information

Actual comparative health plan data from the 1996 OMAP Client
Satisfaction Survey were included on the scorecard prototype. The
survey instrument had been developed through a collaborative
effort between the Medicaid agency and consortium members (see
Chapter Six for a detailed discussion of the survey process).

Of the sixty-one items on the survey, satisfaction data were
selected from each of four domains of interest: overall health plan sat-

isfaction, provider-level satisfaction, ratings of access-related issues, and satisfaction with availability of information. Summary tables were included on the scorecard at varying levels of detail, and focus group facilitators probed for their respective utility and comprehensiveness.

Clinical Performance Measures

Although round one and other focus group research had found that population-based clinical performance measures were of limited use to consumers, we chose to include three HEDIS measures on the scorecard prototype. We wanted to probe for their relevance in the context of a scorecard document. We selected two alternative formats to display the HEDIS scores: (1) as stand-alone pages with a brief explanation of the measure and why it was important and (2) in the context of a "health event scenario" maternity care. The three HEDIS measures selected covered a broad range of audiences, from young families (maternity care and childhood immunizations) to individuals with a chronic condition (diabetes).

Health Event Scenario

A unique feature of the Oregon prototype scorecard was the health event scenario. This component of the scorecard grew from our desire to find a way to use the scorecard as an educational tool for consumers in terms of amplifying the meaning of HEDIS measures by embedding them in a familiar context. In so doing, HEDIS measures were nested in other data sources, so that the resulting product was a comprehensive picture of a health event that included multiple sources of information. These sources combined consumer-derived information (perceptions of quality of care from self-reported satisfaction ratings) with health-plan-derived measures (service features and HEDIS scores). Although maternity care was selected for the prototype, this feature could be employed for a range of health conditions, depending on the population of interest.

Round Two: Information Presentation

From a presentation standpoint, the guiding principle of the consortium was to create a user-friendly scorecard format. Round one participants made it clear that they often found themselves overwhelmed with too much information that was inconsistently displayed and not directed at their concerns. In the second round of focus groups, we presented a variety of formats and probed for participants' preferences among them. For both the satisfaction ratings and the HEDIS scores, we included bar graphs (with and without percentages), ovals shaded to indicate high, medium, and low scores (with and without percentages), and matrices with percentages. Each was presented and discussed from a user's perspective. In addition to the paper-based prototype materials, participants reviewed and discussed the utility of videos, computers, and an accessible 800–number telephone advice line.

The responses of participants to the various formats pointed us toward three groups of presentation issues that have a significant effect on how desired information can be successfully displayed in a scorecard context. Careful organization of information is essential. Avoiding information overload without omitting important data is a constant challenge. Staying with familiar terms and graphics makes complex information more useful. A fourth element emerged from these discussions that is not a format issue: access to an informed person to help clarify questions and guide the search for information.

Organization of Information

The arrangement of information is critical to its utility. The complexity of health-insuring organizations requires scorecard designers to take special care to display comparative information without overwhelming users with unnecessary details. The following scorecard elements helped with the task of organizing information efficiently:

Overview of the information. An index or table of contents guides users through the levels of detail contained within a scorecard. This index should allow users to focus on areas of highest interest while avoiding getting lost in the details they are not likely to find useful.

Consistent structure. Mixing scores on graphs or numbered tables where *good* is sometimes a high and sometimes a low score is confusing and results in information overload. All scales, graphs, charts, and tables should be clearly presented and consistent in the ways in which they identify and differentiate favorable from unfavorable ratings.

Side-by-side comparisons. Comparable information about different plans should be placed in close proximity to facilitate comparison. The use of tables, graphs, and other illustrative material should clearly indicate where and how health plans differ. A benchmark or standard is a preferred tool for depicting the range of differences among plans as well as grounding each score to a "gold standard."

Information Reduction

As with the organization of information, density and volume are factors that must be addressed in all aspects of scorecard development. Whenever possible, distilling complex information into bite-size pieces is a worthy goal.

High-medium-low rankings. It is preferable to identify the mean or median score among plans being compared so that the user can clearly identify which scores are above and which are below average. For example, positioning a line across a bar chart to identify the average of the scores can be a useful display element.

Customized organization and rankings. The computer excels at helping consumers fit information to their own needs and interests. A well-designed worksheet will help users keep track of their individual assessments and priority scoring of the comparative information presented. Additionally, trained telephone counselors can successfully assist consumers in this activity.

Familiar Language and Symbols

As far as possible, information should be presented in a manner that is compatible with consumers' usual ways of thinking.

Easy-to-understand text. As a rule, large print should used. Medical or technical terms should be avoided where possible. When they are used, they should be explained. Among focus group participants, some found descriptive information in paragraph format easier to understand. Others preferred yes-no tables, noting that patterns of difference that got lost in paragraphs were more evident when presented in a dichotomous (yes-no) format.

Simple graphs. A scorecard should avoid informational clutter. In the same vein, reporting the full distribution of a rating (not only *very good* and *excellent* but also *fair* and *poor*) is recommended so that users can focus on the end of the continuum most important to them. It was also noted that colors and patterns can be helpful, while some graphics (for example, ovals shaded to represent high, medium, and low scores) are not sufficiently detailed to be of much use to some consumers.

Precision of numbers versus percentages. Some focus group participants reported that they trusted numbers, whereas others reported that even simple numbers and statistics were confusing. Further, symbols based on statistics, for example, black as significantly *above average* and white as significantly *below average*, were felt to mask too much detail for some users. Associating a percentage or number with a symbol is a way of visualizing a statistic, thus providing a greater level of detail. This combined presentation was preferred by many consumers.

User control. Computers as presentation vehicles were generally regarded as helpful, although some consumers found them intimidating. But computers allow users to weigh the relative importance of rating factors with greater ease, lets them go back to previous screens, makes a "help" button available, and lets them print out selected sections. These features combined to give the computer high ratings as a choice tool for consumers.

Mixing media. Multiple forms of media (print, telephone, video, computer) for presenting comparative information are helpful. As these media are made available, care should be taken to ensure that language and data presentation are consistent across all formats.

Informed Person

In addition to the media alternatives presented and discussed, focus group participants consistently expressed a strong preference for access to an informed person to consult with in the interpretation of measures and other information presented on a scorecard. Group orientation meetings with an informed counselor was also a recommended strategy. This personal access is an important supportive function to integrate with any and all media formats used in consumer scorecard designs.

Recommendations for Future Scorecard Design

Numerous broad conclusions derive from our focus groups for future scorecard design. A consumer-oriented scorecard ought to be different from a scorecard designed for benefits coordinators in large firms or volume purchasing agents. Both the content and the format should reflect these differences.

Attend to Consumer Goals of Choice and Voice

Consumers appreciate the support for self-directed choice and individual feedback built into a consumer-oriented scorecard. They are delighted with the opportunity to send focused messages to health plans about quality and satisfaction that are less dramatic than leaving their chosen health plan to make a point. Rural residents and employees in firms with no choice have no other options; disenrolling is not an available market strategy for large numbers of consumers. Persons with disabilities and chronic health conditions are loathe to leave a plan in which they get generally satisfactory service, in spite of those aspects of care in which service is less than satisfactory. For these consumers, disenrollment is a last resort. Consumers with extraordinary health care needs want to have an efficient way to provide feedback to health plans about service quality, with a reasonable assurance that this feedback will be acted upon in a positive fashion.

Give Unbiased Information

Consumers want an independent, unbiased source of comparative information rather than the current option of having to rely on the marketing materials produced by individual health plans.

Keep Information Relevant

Information *content* and *display* should converge to clarify relevance in a scorecard's design. Whichever data are included in whatever format, a consumer scorecard should pass the test of being useful for decision-making purposes. Real differences among health plans must be displayed clearly. Information that is not relevant to the choice task should be eliminated. Scorecards should be sufficiently comprehensive, while including only the information necessary for making choices. Scorecard designers need to struggle with the paradox of information: relevant information becomes obscured in a field of excessive information.

Customize Information

Information needs vary across categories of persons. For this reason, tailoring information to specific consumer audiences will be a requirement in producing a truly useful scorecard. Computers excel at giving consumers control over this function, although a carefully constructed paper scorecard and worksheet can assist consumers in the task of organizing complex information to fit their individual circumstance for making a health plan choice.

Attend to Audience

Information content and display features must be compatible with the cognitive processing tasks associated with choice decisions. In simpler terms, comparative information must be meaningful to its intended audience. The language, symbols, and graphics used on a scorecard must relate to the experience and educational levels of scorecard users. For example, bar charts with error bars may be quite familiar to researchers and statisticians, but the general public may be confused by "those little things sticking off the ends of the bars."

Be Consistent

Great care needs to be exercised in maintaining consistency of vocabulary and the symbolic representations of quality across scorecard sections and indicators. This is particularly the case if different media are used to present similar information.

Make Scorecard Accessible

Access includes both physical and psychological dimensions. Comparative scorecard information must be retrievable at places and times when choice decisions are to be made. Scorecards and related information should be geographically tailored and available, preferably in widely accessible public places (public libraries, health care facilities, and other public venues). Scorecard designers need to be aware of sensory obstacles and respond with appropriate media such as Braille and print size (for persons with visual impairments). Also, they should communicate complex information as simply as possible for persons with cognitive impairments.

The Promise of Scorecards

The notion of a consumer scorecard holds great promise. It promises access to reliable and valid information about differences in how health plans serve their members; it promises a vehicle for facilitating choice; it promises a feedback loop from consumers to health plans and providers; cumulatively, it promises a mechanism for quality improvement in health services delivery.

Scorecards can also quickly become a marketing tool, one among the many that already exist. Marketing information provides consumers with what health plans think consumers ought to hear rather than expressions of consumer-driven preferences for the quality and choice information they need to make informed health plan decisions.

The many promises will be hard to realize. Soliciting, analyzing, and reporting reliable, comparative health plan information will most likely be costly, labor-intensive, and time consuming. Oregon consumers reminded us of the costs involved and raised questions about whether the benefits justified these costs. The dual goals of *choice* and *voice* should guide further scorecard development activities in both the public and private health care sectors.

References

Benova, Inc. "Choice Care: A Medicaid/Medicare Consumers Values/Preferences and Report Care Model for Health Plan Selection." Report to Agency for Health Care Policy and Research, Contract No. 282–94–2031, 1995.

Krueger, R. A. *Focus Groups, A Practical Guide for Applied Research.* Thousand Oaks, Calif.: Sage, 1988.

Chapter Five

Tailoring Choice Information to Special Populations

Pamela P. Hanes

There are many ways to define a special population. *Special* denotes something exceptional, distinct, or unique to a class of individuals. When speaking of special populations in the context of health care, we usually refer to a group of people who have a commonly identified set of health care needs.

Examples of special-need population groups include high-risk pregnant women, substance abusers, persons with significant disabilities, or those with chronic and persistent mental illness. Other subgroups have unique social characteristics from which health care needs emerge: families living in poverty, frail elders living alone, non-English-speaking individuals, and uninsured children.

For the purposes of the Oregon Consumer Scorecard Project, particular attention was paid to the information preferences of two special-need populations—individuals with significant chronic illnesses and disabilities* and those living in rural areas of the state. Our working hypothesis was that these individuals would express qualitatively different needs for choice information.

---

*In this context, "significant" denoted a chronic condition or disability that interferes with an individual's ability to engage in age-appropriate activities. Examples include a child's ability to learn or engage in school-related activities, an adult's ability to engage in gainful employment, or an older person's ability to perform routine activities of daily living. In addition to functional impairment, "significant" was defined as having extraordinary health care needs beyond routine and episodic care, including personal assistance, frequent hospitalizations, and the need for durable medical equipment and therapies.

We reviewed previous research on patient satisfaction among special populations related to both managed care and fee-for-service health insurance to assess the extent to which special need would influence overall consumer satisfaction and how the interaction of these factors might affect choice decisions.

There were only a few studies of how special populations were faring under managed care and fewer still on how special need might be translated into quality and performance measurement. Aside from the focus group research already reviewed in Chapter Four, which was primarily done in Oregon, we had few clues about what health plan performance information would be of greatest interest to consumers with extraordinary health care needs.

Special Population Perspectives

As noted throughout this volume, consumers are interested in hearing assessments of health plans from people in their own circumstances when it comes to choosing a health plan. This *reference group* factor was a critical consideration in the design and pilot-testing of our prototype scorecard materials. The sections that follow describe examples the consortium considered in designing the prototype scorecard materials.

Life Course

Within this framework, *special* is defined on the basis of where in the life cycle groups of individuals reside, for example, infants and children, adolescents and young adults, women of childbearing years, or middle-age and older adults. A life course perspective is reflected in the performance measures developed under the aegis of the NCQA Medicaid HEDIS Workgroup, where health plan performance measures were heavily weighted toward women of childbearing age and children because these groups make up the largest eligibility category in the Medicaid program.

Sociodemographic Status

This perspective has numerous applications, depending on the social or demographic characteristic of interest. A demographic framework is amenable to two-way comparisons, where the comparison group constitutes the majority population. For example, health plan performance can be compared between individuals who are employed and privately insured relative to persons who are receiving public assistance and Medicaid. These pairwise comparisons are appropriate for providing a reference group, or standard, to which vulnerable populations' satisfaction, access, and outcomes ratings can be compared.

Demographic characteristics are often linked to health and functional status because of the strong correlation between poverty, ill health, and disability. Notably, impoverished children are especially vulnerable to the health risks associated with substandard housing, inadequate sanitation, poor diets, and otherwise high-stress environments. In many respects, the most vulnerable among us need the closest scrutiny to ensure that the health care system meets their needs.

Health and Functional Status

Prior research has shown that self-assessed health status is a valid measure of actual health status, accurately predicting health care utilization. Further, a growing body of evidence suggests a relationship between health care use and overall consumer satisfaction. For example, studies have found that people who assess their health as *good* or *excellent* tend to be more satisfied with their health care than individuals with chronic health conditions or other extraordinary health care needs.

Special Populations and Performance Measurement

Gold (1994) suggests looking at a wide range of available data to find clues about how special populations perceive and assess the value and quality of the health care services they receive. He argues that the interaction of variables found in multiple data sources provides the most complete picture of how individual and group differences will influence personal expectations and satisfaction with health care delivery. He includes the following types of data: demographics, individual behavior and health practices, perceptions of self, attributes of health care systems and providers, social and political events, and health care utilization histories.

A number of factors influence the data collected from special populations, including culture-based health beliefs and behaviors, health-seeking behaviors that affect perceptions of access as well as use of health services, literacy levels, and unique interpretations of verbal, auditory, and visual cues and information.

The findings from a study by Fox, Wicks, Kelly, and Greaney (1990), who monitored the experiences of children with special needs in managed care organizations, highlight several issues that are noteworthy for scorecard development. These issues relate to service provision, benefit design, and comprehensiveness of coverage (see also Fox, Wicks, and Newacheck, 1993; Newacheck, Hughes, Stoddard, and Halfon, 1994; Hanes, Ostherr, and Stevens, 1995; Kanthor, Pless, Satterwhite, and Myers, 1974; Mauldon and others, 1994; Okamoto and Shurtleff, 1981). It is evident from these studies that parents are eager for reliable comparative information about how well plans are performing along these dimensions.

The health care needs of chronically ill or disabled children are complex and require a highly coordinated, multidisciplinary approach to care management. The ability of plans to provide or arrange for specialists from a range of disciplines is an important organizational feature to monitor at the health plan level.

The same is true for adults with mental or cognitive impairments and disabilities. It has been suggested that capitated managed care may lead to better integration of mental health and medical care services, better coordination between mental health and medical care providers, and improved quality of care. As with children who have special health care needs, adults with physical and mental impairments require an enhanced range of services and entry points into the service system (Christianson and others, 1992; Lehman, 1987; Lurie and others, 1992; Taube, Goldman, and Salkever, 1990).

Whether or not particular therapies and long-term supports are part of a benefit package, managed care organizations have both financial and quality incentives to promote care coordination among the range of services providers with whom these patients interact.

Special Needs of Rural Consumers

The social, demographic, and resource factors related to rural health care consumers should also be considered in the development of consumer choice information materials. The fundamental task of presenting comparative health plan and provider information that reflects available health plans has not been adequately dealt with in previous scorecard efforts. Because earlier scorecard projects had been targeted primarily at volume purchasers, presenting information that is relevant and tailored to individual consumers had received little attention.

We know that rural, as opposed to urban, populations are more likely to consider themselves in fair or poor health, are less likely to engage in preventive behaviors (for example, wearing seat belts or getting regular exercise), have higher rates of disability, and participate less in regular screening services.

The available data about rural Americans also suggest that they are less likely to be insured, less likely to have contact with physicians, and more likely to be hospitalized than people who live in urban areas. Travel time to hospitals and physicians and restricted availability and access to specialty care serve to confound issues of satisfaction and perceived performance of health plans, especially for heavy users.

Hanes, Ostherr, and Stevens (1995) found access and satisfaction to be highly correlated in a rural sample of parents of children with special health care needs in Oregon. In all categories of health services, rural families reported more difficulty obtaining health care than families living in urban and suburban areas of the state. For specialty care, there was a four-fold difference in reported level of difficulty in securing specialist care. Similar patterns of difference were reported for the various therapies that special-needs children required, including physical, occupational, and speech therapies.

Likewise, when level of satisfaction was examined for urban-rural differences, significant differences appeared. The authors found a strong association between access and satisfaction; the more difficult the service was to obtain the less satisfied parents were with it. The one notable exception was primary care, where access was generally assessed to be equal between rural and urban respondents. Yet, three times as many rural families expressed dissatisfaction with the primary care they received.

Perhaps the most important factor in thinking about the uniqueness of rural consumers, in terms of scorecard development, is the lack of availability of health resources found in most rural areas. In designing an information dissemination strategy built on choice preferences, this restricted choice is an omnipresent factor to be reconciled in presenting useful performance, access, and satisfaction information to rural consumers.

The Challenges Summarized

Population subgroups, as well as different constituencies (consumers, purchasers, physicians, policymakers), have varying perceptions about what constitutes quality. As discussed in Chapter Four, it is important to recognize and account for these perceptual differences in the reporting of comparative quality information; what is presented should be tailored to the particular information preferences, cognitive level, and definitional assumptions of the target audience.

From a measurement perspective, most significant chronic conditions and disabilities are low-incidence occurrences within the general population. Even when scorecard designers can develop efficient methods for providing condition-specific information on a subpopulation basis, measuring satisfaction and outcomes by health plan is a special challenge because the numbers in the groups are small and measurement costs are high. Likewise, in most rural areas population is sparse. Therefore, providing health plan performance information to rural consumers that is geographically sensitive will involve added costs and methodological creativity.

References

Christianson, J., and others. "Use of Community-Based Mental Health Programs by HMOs: Evidence from a Medicaid Demonstration." *American Journal of Public Health,* 1992, 82(9), 970–796.

Fox, H. B., Wicks, L. B., Kelly, R. W., and Greaney, A. "An Examination of HMO Policies Affecting Children and Adolescents: A Briefing Report." Fox Health Policy Consultants, Washington, D.C., Sept. 1990.

Fox, H., Wicks, L., and Newacheck, P. "State Medicaid Health Maintenance Organization Policies and Special Needs Children." *Health Care Financing Review,* Fall 1993.

Gold, R. "Collecting Information from Groups with Special Needs." Draft report prepared for the Agency for Health Care Policy and Research under contract to Health Systems Research, Inc., Contract No. 282–91–0027, 1994.

Hanes, P., Ostherr, K., and Stevens, D. "Oregon Statewide Needs Assessment for Children with Special Health Care Needs." Oregon Health Policy Institute, Oregon Health Sciences University, Portland, Oreg., Mar. 1995.

Kanthor, H., Pless, B., Satterwhite, B., and Myers, G. "Areas of Responsibility in the Health Care of Multiply Handicapped Children." *Pediatrics,* 1974, 54(6), 779–785.

Lehman, A. "Capitation Payment and Mental Health Care: A Review of the Opportunities and Risks." *Hospital and Community Psychiatry,* Jan. 1987, pp. 31–38.

Lurie, N., and others. "Does Capitation Affect the Health of the Chronically Mentally Ill?" *Journal of the American Medical Association, 267*(24), 1992, 3300–3304.

Mauldon, J., and others. "Rationing or Rationalizing Children's Medical Care: Comparison of a Medicaid HMO with Fee-for-Service Care." *American Journal of Public Health,* 1994, 84(6), 899–904.

Newacheck, P., Hughes, J., Stoddard, J., and Halfon, N. "Children with Chronic Illness and Medicaid Managed Care." *Pediatrics*, 1994, 93(3), 497–500.
Okamoto, G. A., and Shurtleff, D. A. "Perceived First Contact Care for Disabled Children." *Pediatrics*, 1981, 67(4), 530–535.
Taube, C., Goldman, H., and Salkever, D. "Medicaid Coverage for Mental Illness: Balancing Access and Costs." *Health Affairs*, 1990, 9(1), 5–18.

Chapter Six

Eliciting, Measuring, and Reporting Consumer Satisfaction

Christine Edlund

In the dynamic restructuring of health care delivery in America, choice *is* expanding, but the expanded alternatives are not of consistent quality. There is an inherent incentive within highly competitive managed health care markets to provide less care or to compromise quality in order to control costs. The tendency to contain costs at the expense of quality is mitigated, in part, by the professional ethics of health care providers and by the ability of consumers to "vote with their feet" through disenrollment and reenrollment decisions. But consumers cannot be prudent purchasers of health care without good information. An important aspect of informed decision making is the availability of reliable and personally relevant comparative health plan information.

In previous chapters, the authors have discussed what consumers *want* and *need to know* in order to make informed choices among the varied insurance products available to them. A key finding from the Oregon Consumer Scorecard Project was that consumers found it extremely difficult to navigate through complex health care organizations (Hanes and Greenlick, 1996). Further, consumers needed clear and unambiguous information about how plans actually work. For example, health plan members want specific information about available primary care providers before selecting their own provider. Persons with chronic health conditions reported needing explicit and consistent information about the processes that plans use for accessing specialty care and ancillary goods and services.

Focus group participants in Oregon noted that having enrollee satisfaction data about the accessibility and responsiveness of health care providers and quality of plan services would be of high utility in choosing a health plan (Hanes and Greenlick, 1996). An efficient way to obtain this type of consumer feedback is through a carefully designed and independently conducted health plan consumer satisfaction survey.

Consumer Satisfaction Measures

Consumer satisfaction measures are qualitatively different from clinical process and outcomes measurement in that they quantify a user's perceptions of quality rather than measure clinical performance. Studies have shown that satisfied patients tend to participate more fully in their treatment regimens and consequently have better clinical outcomes (Pascoe, 1983). Ware, Snyder, Wright, and Davies (1983) found a strong relationship between consumer satisfaction and the decision to change health care providers. More recent research on the health-care-seeking behavior of poor, urban residents showed that 24 percent of those who had seen a physician delayed seeking care at some time because they were dissatisfied with how long it took to get an appointment (Kiefe and Hyman, 1996). These varied findings suggest that consumer satisfaction is an important component of monitoring health plan performance and thus should be included in any comparative reporting mechanism developed.

Until recently, data from consumer satisfaction surveys have been used by hospital systems and health plans for internal quality improvement and marketing purposes. Sometimes, survey instruments are brief, perhaps having only two questions: How did we do? and What could we do to improve? Other surveys are long, with as many as one hundred detailed questions. Ideally, enrollee satisfaction data collected and presented on a consumer scorecard should include more than responses to a few brief questions and less than the responses from the long, detailed surveys needed to gain feedback on a specific clinical encounter.

A major challenge to developing consumer satisfaction surveys for scorecard purposes is that of choosing salient indicators of *quality, access,* and *service* that provide not only reliable and valid data but also have utility from a consumer perspective. An additional challenge is the dynamic nature of the change that is occurring in the very health care organizations that are being assessed. The effect of this dynamism is that consumers' assessments of their plans along a number of critical dimensions can quickly become obsolete because they do not reflect the structural changes as they occur. Changes in ownership and administrative relationships are but two of a range of organizational attributes that are in a constant state of flux in today's market. As a result, the range, scope, and timing of information required to keep pace with these changes can be daunting.

Efforts to collect and report consumer satisfaction data should enlist the participation of all affected stakeholders, thereby minimizing the potential for challenges to the data's validity and ultimate utility at the scorecard production stage. Stakeholder involvement can take several forms—from key informant interviews to focus groups to detailed committee work. Based on our experience, it is advisable to use a consensus process whenever possible while, at the same time, maintaining the appropriate rigor and integrity of conventional scientific methods in the collection, analysis, and reporting of the data.

Input from all affected stakeholders is important; it ensures buy-in and ownership of the final scorecard product. If successfully implemented, each of the multiple audiences involved should substantially benefit from their participation in the process.

Construction of a Consumer Satisfaction Survey

In 1995, the Office of Medical Assistance Programs (OMAP)—Oregon's Medicaid agency—began the development of its 1996 Consumer Satisfaction Survey of eligible individuals and families enrolled in the Oregon Health Plan Medicaid program. Because the OHP-Medicaid program was authorized under a federal waiver,

OMAP was required to establish accountability mechanisms that would demonstrate improvement in health care access and in the health status of Oregonians served by the program. In particular, these accountability measures were to track and document the extent of increased access to primary care and preventive services and to monitor the quality and cost-effectiveness of care provided. To fulfill this accountability mandate, OMAP developed a comprehensive quality assurance program that included consumer satisfaction surveys.

The Oregon Consumer Scorecard Consortium

As OMAP was initiating plans for its survey, the Oregon Consumer Scorecard Consortium was completing its work plan for prototype scorecard development. The consortium afforded a unique opportunity for OMAP to design and implement a useful, methodologically sound survey instrument in partnership with a broad-based group of stakeholders. These stakeholders included consumer advocates, the health plans participating in the OHP-Medicaid program, and other affected state agencies and professional groups. The consortium, through its technical, health plan, and consumer committees, provided a collaborative environment for the development of a satisfaction survey instrument and prototype scorecard materials that attended uniquely to the needs of each constituency.

Early in the collaboration, Oregon scorecard planners addressed several policy issues preparatory to designing the consumer satisfaction survey. These issues had direct implications for the subsequent prototype scorecard materials to be developed. The issues were as follows:

• *Defining the lines of business.* Health insurers and insurance or provider organizations typically market multiple insurance products (for example, HMOs, PPOs, point-of-service plans) and have both

Medicaid and Medicare lines of business. Decisions about whether to include all products and lines of business in a scorecard effort were addressed early in the survey design process.

• *Attention to market areas.* Most health plans market their products in several counties. It was important to recognize that provider and delivery system characteristics differ by market and geographical area, in particular, between rural and urban markets. Given the potential for significant differences based on the resource capacity of the market area, it was important that the survey sampling methods reflect this reality.

• *Attention to special populations.* Various subgroups of a health plan's membership (for example, individuals with chronic health conditions) use health care services differently. Small population subgroups required special consideration as we developed the survey sampling plan to ensure that their voices were appropriately included in the plan's satisfaction ratings.

The remainder of this chapter discusses how these issues were effectively managed and integrated into the design and conduct of a comprehensive consumer satisfaction survey; their implications for reporting comparative survey findings are also discussed.

Surveying a Medicaid Population

Collecting consumer satisfaction data from a Medicaid population can be a challenging enterprise. To begin, the traditional Medicaid population is socially and economically disadvantaged in several ways. By definition, its members live well below the federal poverty level (in most states), are less educated than the general population, tend to be highly mobile, and frequently do not speak English. Although these demographic factors are not confined to a Medicaid population, their prevalence among Medicaid recipients is higher. To design a survey that effectively reaches the target population, planners had to deal with these practical issues.

Survey Methods

Primary survey methods include mail-back and telephone surveys; there are advantages and disadvantages to both methods. The telephone survey, with multiple call-backs, yields the highest response rate in a relatively short period of time. However, aside from the higher cost, there are two disadvantages to the telephone survey for consumer satisfaction research. The first is that telephone surveys can result in inflated satisfaction scores (Hall, 1995). Telephone survey respondents report a hesitancy to make negative statements to a telephone interviewer. The second and more important disadvantage is the bias that is introduced if respondents in the sample population do not have a telephone or are highly mobile and frequently have their telephones disconnected. A survey research firm in Portland reported that in their administration of a telephone survey to OHP-Medicaid members for a local health plan, approximately 40 percent of plan enrollees were unreachable by telephone for one of these reasons.

The mail-back survey has the advantage of greater perceived privacy. As a result, respondents are more likely to answer questions in a way that reflects their true feelings. The major disadvantage of a mail-back survey is nonresponder bias. For a Medicaid population, this problem is significant. In a review of Medicaid client satisfaction surveys nationwide, the National Committee for Quality Assurance (NCQA) found mail-back response rates ranging from 25 to 35 percent.

Response rates of less than 50 percent are considered marginal for analytical purposes because of the threats to validity imposed by nonresponder bias (Babbie, 1995). With these limitations in mind, and given the expense and other disadvantages of a telephone survey, OMAP decided to administer a multiple-stage, mail-back consumer satisfaction survey in January of 1996. Because a key element of OMAP's quality assurance program was the consumer satisfaction survey, it was important to maximize the response rate while generating reliable and valid data.

The 1996 Medicaid Client Satisfaction Survey

At the time the survey was being developed, all managed care plans doing business in Oregon were serving the OHP-Medicaid population. By law, these health plans were required to offer an identical benefit package to OHP-Medicaid enrollees. Further, at the time there were no co-payment or premium requirements for enrollees. The absolute comparability of the benefit package and absence of any differential cost sharing made the OHP-Medicaid population a circumscribed, manageable population to target for prototype scorecard development purposes.

Early in the instrument development process, it was agreed that the following conditions would need to be met in the survey's design:

• The survey would be readable by people with no more than a sixth-grade reading level (an existing OMAP requirement of all materials sent out to the OHP-Medicaid population).

• The survey would be anchored in time—a technique developed specifically for health surveys and included in a range of bounded recall procedures (Aday, 1996; Sudman, Finn, and Lannom, 1984). The time anchor would be used to avoid memory lapses about specific events or perceptions of care; the longer the time frame for which a respondent is asked to recall, the more likely it is that the individual's perceptions will become skewed. In our case, respondents were asked to respond to questions about care received within the previous six months.

• The survey would contain population-relevant measures that were jargon-free and written in a user-friendly format.

• Comparability with previous OMAP surveys would be sought, at least for a core set of questions.

It should be noted that these factors are equally important in designing a survey for a commercially insured population. Many existing survey instruments are designed at a much higher reading level and contain jargon and confusing terms. Additionally, in capturing the issues that are of concern to special populations, it is appropriate to consider separate modules in addition to a core set of questions.

The issue of comparability between surveys and over time is a significant one. Not only is the health care industry changing rapidly but so too are the methods and technology used in survey research. Strategies used to increase response rates are becoming increasingly refined and perfected. Every instrument revision or change in method (for example, replacing a phone survey with a mail-back) limits the comparability of results over time. Original design decisions should be carefully considered with these factors in mind, as every alteration to a survey will have consequences for future analysis.

Readability

The American Association of Health Plans (formerly the Group Health Association of America [GHAA]) Client Satisfaction Survey served as OMAP's baseline survey instrument. It was administered just prior to the implementation of the OHP-Medicaid program in 1994. The GHAA survey instrument was written at a tenth-grade reading level, but it was chosen because of its widespread use nationally with commercial populations. Only in retrospect did OMAP fully appreciate that reading level would be such a significant barrier to completion with its Medicaid population.

A sizable number of respondents to the baseline survey noted that they did not understand many of the questions. Even though this instrument had been used extensively with commercially insured populations, it contained serious comprehension barriers for elementary-level readers. For example, the instructions at the beginning of a set of questions read, "Thinking about your own health care, how would you rate the following?" This statement was then followed by a set of categorical responses such as "availability of medical information or advice by phone." This type of question construction requires the respondent to refer back to the original statement for each categorical option; it proved to be confusing, often resulting in skipped or internally inconsistent responses.

For the 1996 survey, OMAP transformed each of these questions into a complete sentence so that the respondent need not remember the original instructions for each subsequent question. Additionally, the project staff agreed to incorporate revisions suggested in NCQA's draft Medicaid Satisfaction Survey, as well as other modifications suggested by OMAP staff and the consortium technical committee. Ultimately, the instrument was readable at a 5.9-grade level, as assessed with the Flesch-Kincaid Grade Level Assessment (available in many word processing software packages). Sample questions are shown in Exhibit 6.1.

Another major component of readability is *understandability*. Many surveys are complex in their design, with repeated skip patterns and screens. For a Medicaid population in particular, these commonly used design features of written surveys should be used sparingly, although their judicious use can be equally challenging. Avoiding screens altogether will result in an instrument on which every question could conceivably have a response category with some form of "does not apply to me." This structure can be monotonous and boring to the respondent. Repeatedly reading questions that do not apply often leads respondents to not complete their surveys or, worse yet, to not returning them at all.

Exhibit 6.1. Sample Questions.

Thinking about your health plan, how would you rate the following? (Mark one square on each line.)

	Poor	Fair	Good	Very Good	Excellent
9. Rate your health plan's coverage for preventive care and general checkups.	❑	❑	❑	❑	❑
10. Rate your health plan's coverage for illness visits and treatments.	❑	❑	❑	❑	❑
11. Rate the number of primary care doctors or clinics you have to choose from with your health plan.	❑	❑	❑	❑	❑

For the 1996 survey, OMAP chose to incorporate two skip patterns, or screens. After answering some basic questions about their health plan and experience with their health plan, respondents were asked if they had seen their primary care provider in the last six months. If they had, they were instructed to continue through a battery of access and provider satisfaction questions. If they had not, they were skipped to the end of the survey to answer some general questions regarding possible barriers to care and demographic information. In all, there were two of these skip instructions on the entire survey of sixty-one questions. Survey skip questions are shown in Exhibit 6.2.

Indicators of Satisfaction

The GHAA survey instrument divided the key satisfaction indicators into three general domains: (1) satisfaction with health care services and providers; (2) general satisfaction with care; and (3) satisfaction with health plan. A series of indicators were included in each of these three areas, based on previously established reliability and validity tests confirming their measurement of satisfaction domains (Davies and Ware, 1991). The 1996 OMAP survey contained twelve of the thirteen domains from the GHAA survey. (OMAP dropped the financial arrangement section because it was not applicable to the population.) The domains included the following:

- Accessibility and availability of services and providers
- Technical quality

Exhibit 6.2. Survey Skip Instructions.

The next questions are about your experiences in the last 6 months only.

20. During the last 6 months, did you (not a family member) make any visits to a doctor or nurse who is covered by your health plan? (Mark one square.)

  ❏ No   ☞   If no, please skip to Question 47.

  ❏ Yes   ☞   If yes, please go to Question 21.

- Interpersonal dimensions of care
- Communication
- Choice and continuity
- Health plan communication
- Outcomes of care
- Coverage

Recent research findings suggest that provider-specific indicators are very important to Medicaid patients because they see provider attitudes and communication styles as a reflection of the level of respect paid to them. Further, these feelings of respect affect how Medicaid patients evaluate other aspects of their health care experience (Baldasare, 1995).

Additional questions that were added to the 1996 survey because they were felt to strongly influence satisfaction were as follows:

- Length of time continuously enrolled in health plan (Q2)
- How the client became enrolled in the health plan (Q3)
- Information used in making the decision about which plan to choose (Q4)
- Availability of translation and transportation services (Q48)
- Change of address (Q59)

Sample questions are shown in Exhibit 6.3.

Finally, questions relating to self-assessed health status, changes in health status, and presence of a range of chronic conditions (each from the SF–36 Health Survey [Ware, 1993]) were added as possible control variables for the analysis.

The Survey Sampling Plan

The 1996 survey was designed to assess overall satisfaction with access and health care services of OHP-Medicaid enrollees, as well as

Exhibit 6.3. Influencing Factors Added in 1996.

2. How many months or years **in a row** have you been in **your health plan?**
    (*Mark one square*)
    ❑ Less than 6 months
    ❑ At least 6 months, but less than 1 year
    ❑ At least 1 year, but less than 2 years
    ❑ At least 2 years, but less than 3 years
    ❑ More than 3 years
    ❑ Don't know

3. How were you enrolled in **your health plan?** (*Mark one square*)
    ❑ I was in this plan in the past.
    ❑ It was the only one in my area.
    ❑ I had more than one plan to pick from, and I picked this one.
    ❑ I was placed in it.
    ❑ Don't know.
    ❑ Some other way (*please tell us how*) _____

4. If you picked your plan yourself, which of the following
    helped you the most? (*Mark one square*)
    ❑ My doctor helped me decide.
    ❑ A neighbor, friend, or family member helped me decide.
    ❑ I used the information given to me with my application.
    ❑ I didn't pick a health plan.
    ❑ Other (*please tell us*) _____

48. Why weren't you able to get the health care services **you wanted or needed**
    through your health plan? (*Mark all squares that apply*)
    ❑ I had trouble finding a doctor or nurse in my local area
       that would see me.
    ❑ The health care service I wanted wasn't covered by my health plan.
    ❑ Physical problems made it difficult for me to get to the office or clinic.
    ❑ The doctor or nurse that I saw before isn't part of my health plan.
    ❑ It is easier to see a doctor or nurse who isn't part of my health plan.
    ❑ I didn't like my choice of doctors or nurses.
    ❑ I was not able to get a ride.
    ❑ I don't understand English very well.
    ❑ Other (*please tell us*) _____

59. Have you moved in last 6 months? (*Mark one square*)
    ❑ No
    ❑ Yes

the satisfaction ratings of certain subgroups within the larger population. The internal quality assurance needs of OMAP, coupled with the information needs of the consortium for comparative health plan ratings, required a sampling plan that allowed for subgroup analysis.

Sampling Frame. Fourteen of the eighteen health plans participating in the OHP-Medicaid program met the enrollment criteria of at least one thousand adult OHP-Medicaid members (between the ages of eighteen and sixty-four years) who had been continuously enrolled in the health plan for at least six months.

Response rates for a Medicaid population are generally low, so the selected sample size of one thousand members per plan was a conservative estimate of what it might take to get the desired four hundred responses per plan. For the four plans that did not have one thousand continuously enrolled members, the entire population of six-month, continuously enrolled adults was mailed questionnaires. This sampling strategy was to ensure a sufficient sample per plan to permit reporting comparative scores with a 95 percent confidence level.

Small Numbers. The problem of small sample sizes, particularly when applying a continuous enrollment criterion, is likely to be an issue for any scorecard effort. Great care should be taken to ensure that smaller health plans have adequate numbers if they are to be included in scorecard reports. The number of continuously enrolled members among health plans participating in the OHP-Medicaid program ranged from 297 to 24,500 in 1995.

Subgroup Analysis. OMAP was interested in an analysis that would include individual Medicaid eligibility categories; therefore, this factor also had to be incorporated into the sampling strategy. The OHP-Medicaid program not only increased coverage to 120,000 previously uninsured Oregonians, it also shifted large numbers of the traditional Medicaid population into managed care organizations.

Only 30 percent of the Medicaid population in Oregon was enrolled in a managed care health plan prior to the implementation of the Oregon Health Plan, so a major shift to managed care happened in 1994. It was important to OMAP to learn whether managed care organizations were providing services perceived to be at least equal in quality to those previously provided in a fee-for-service system.

A simple random sample of all eligibility categories would have captured adequate numbers of the largest group within OHP-Medicaid at the time—the Aid to Dependent Children (ADC) program. However, the number of enrolled clients in the other categories (pregnant women at or below 133 percent of the federal poverty level and unemployable adults with no dependent children) was much smaller. Therefore, these eligibility categories were oversampled to ensure their adequate representation in the final analysis.

The Rural-Urban Factor. Finally, because Oregon is a rural state with a large number of sparsely populated counties, there was a desire to examine the satisfaction levels in urban, suburban, rural, and frontier market areas separately. In a Medicaid delivery system, market area is defined as county because of the requirement that recipients choose a plan offered in their county of residence.

Defining this geographic factor for sampling and analytical purposes presented a challenge. The most straightforward approach would have been to use the U.S. Bureau of Census definition of metropolitan and nonmetropolitan counties. But these definitions ignore the reality of states like Oregon. Although Oregon has a few metropolitan areas where most of the population lives, the remainder of the state is not homogeneous in terms of degree of rurality. There is a continuum of rurality from "urban" to "rural fringe" (contiguous to and influenced by an urban area) to "rural" to "frontier" (very low population density). These four categories, as defined by population density, have previously been used in health care analysis. The map shown in Exhibit 6.4 displays the dispersion of the population of the state, as well as the number of plans in each county at the time the survey was conducted.

The population density for each geographical unit was as follows:

- Urban: more than one hundred people per square mile
- Rural fringe: between twenty-one and one hundred people per square mile
- Rural: between six and twenty people per square mile
- Frontier: less than six people per square mile

In focus groups conducted as part of the scorecard effort, participants noted that they wanted comparative satisfaction ratings that reflected the opinions of people "like themselves." As one focus group participant stated, "It doesn't do me any good to know how happy people in Portland are with the plans they have to choose from when they are not my choices here in Enterprise!" Therefore, the survey sampling plan included oversampling in rural and frontier areas of the state to ensure that the rural dimension could be included in the analysis.

To summarize, sampling decisions are critical to a well-designed and executed survey, but the complexity of issues surrounding these decisions can be intimidating. Specific factors related to designing a survey sampling strategy for a consumer scorecard should include the following considerations:

Geographic sensitivity. As noted earlier, health plan enrollees are most interested in the satisfaction ratings of people like themselves. This translates into a need to be geographically sensitive when reporting satisfaction scores. For the 1996 OHP-Medicaid survey, our analysis revealed a rural effect on overall satisfaction scores within the same health plan. We did not have large enough individual plan memberships to report urban versus nonurban scores for all participating plans, but we were able to oversample in three of the larger plans and complete this level of analysis.

Lines of business. Most scorecard efforts will not be limited to a Medicaid-only population. Scorecards are more likely to be designed

Exhibit 6.4. Population Density of Oregon Counties (Number of OHP Health Plans by County, 1995).

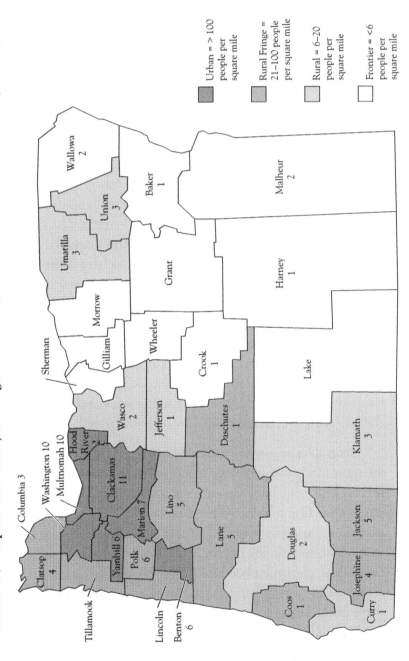

to assist consumers in making choices among the health plans offered by an employer or a purchasing alliance. Employer-sponsored health insurance options often include an HMO product, a preferred provider organization (PPO) product, a point-of-service product (POS), and possibly a traditional indemnity product with varying cost-sharing arrangements. Decisions about which products to be included and compared on the scorecard are numerous and increase the complexity of the enterprise considerably.

Benefits packages. Depending on the employer group, a health plan's HMO product may offer several different benefits packages. They can differ on any or all of the following: co-payments, pharmacy coverage, vision benefits, dental benefits, and other covered services. Although not exhaustive, this list illustrates the complicating factors that can influence the design of a survey and the concurrent production decisions that will follow.

Survey Administration

Having an instrument that is readable and understandable is a critical factor for a successful survey effort, but the best-designed instrument can result in failure if the surveys are not completed and returned. Because mail-back surveys are subject to lower response rates than telephone surveys, focused attention must be exercised to maximize the return rate.

The approach used by OMAP was based on well-established principles and protocols found in the multistep, total design approach (Dillman, 1978), which included the following four steps:

1. *Advance letter mailing.* A personalized letter was sent to each household member in the sample that explained the purpose of the survey and its importance and informed the recipient that he or she would be receiving a survey in the mail the following week.

2. *Initial survey mailing.* The first survey was mailed within a week of the advance letter. This mailing also included a personalized cover letter restating the purpose of the project. The importance

of the cover letter cannot be overstated. Respondents are being asked to give their time to complete the survey, and the letter is the one opportunity the sponsoring organization has to explain the importance of the project. The cover letter should include the following information:

- The importance of the project
- Guarantee of privacy and confidentiality
- Reassurance that the respondent's participation and answers will not affect future benefits or care provided
- Explanation, in lay terms, of how the data will be used and by whom

3. *Follow-up postcard.* The postcard, a reminder about the survey, was mailed one week after the initial survey was mailed. The postcard was mailed to everyone in the sample.

4. *Second survey mailing.* A second copy of the survey was mailed two weeks after the postcard reminder to all nonresponders. The second survey also had an accompanying cover letter.

After a second survey has been mailed, if the response rate is still not at 50 percent, another postcard should be mailed or a reminder call made. At every stage, efforts should be made to keep the survey as personal as possible. Letters should be personalized; postcards should be an attention-getting bright color; and first-class postage should be used at each stage. This is particularly important because not only does first-class mail send a clear message that the recipient is important to the research effort, but bulk mailings can be held at the post office for up to two weeks.

The health plans participating in the consortium provided additional funds so that follow-up telephone prompts could be made to all nonresponders after the second survey was mailed. These calls increased the overall response by an additional 10 percentage points. This multistage mail and phone prompt approach, combined with a strict mailing schedule, resulted in an overall response rate of 63 percent for the 1996 OHP-Medicaid Satisfaction Survey, with a range of 55 to 73 percent among individual health plans.

The timing of each sequence in a mail-back survey is critical. It is preferable to mail on Wednesdays or Thursdays so that the survey arrives on Friday or Saturday. Weekends allow survey recipients a more relaxed period of time in which to fill out the questionnaire. Although most survey researchers recognize the importance of a multistage mailing process, many make compromises in following a tightly constructed schedule—sometimes with unfortunate results.

Presentation of Survey Results

Presentation is the final challenge in the survey process. Previous chapters have discussed the various findings and reporting issues related to the Oregon Consumer Scorecard Consortium's prototype development activities. However, the issues noted here, driven by geography, plan size, and membership characteristics, must also be considered in presenting comparative scorecard data. The easiest adjustments are the straightforward ones: weighting the data to account for geographical oversampling and using finite population corrections for small plans.

For the consortium effort, the decision was also made to separately analyze provider-level and plan-level indicators for presentation purposes. This separate analysis addressed the health plans' concerns about the confounding issue of overlapping provider panels between plans, as well as the fact that plans have less control over provider attitudes and behaviors.

Because the data revealed that the same health plan could have significantly different satisfaction scores in rural areas compared to their urban clinic sites, presentation of the satisfaction data needed to reflect these differences. In some cases, the lower rural scores "depressed" a plan's overall statewide satisfaction ratings. These plans argued that reporting a statewide average disadvantaged them unfairly in terms of the competitiveness of their urban market position. This factor turned out to be a helpful quality assurance tool because it provided finely calibrated information to health plans about where specific service problems lay. Table 6.1 shows the discrepancy in rural and urban scores.

The data from the 1996 survey was presented in separate tables: a nonurban *plan* and *provider* table, with the average of nonurban plan scores for comparison purposes, and separate urban tables, with the same urban comparative benchmark.

Table 6.1. Urban and Rural Scores for the Same Health Plan.

	HMO Oregon	
Satisfaction Indicator	Urban Area Scores (n = 384) %	Rural Area Scores (n = 592) %
Would you recommend your health plan?	79	72
Rate your provider(s) overall.	85	79
Plan Information		
Getting information	41	37
Understanding information	47	45
Plan Coverage		
Coverage for Preventive Services	49	45
Coverage for Illness Visits	50	49
Access and Availability		
Ease of finding a primary care provider	64	66
Specialist referral	49	46
Access to medical care at any time	72	71
Timely primary care provider appointments	71	69
Access to emergency care	66	60
Access to medicines	83	80
Access to advice during office hours	63	59
Access to advice after office hours	45	32
Number of primary care providers to choose from	46	39

Scores reflect "Very Satisfied," which was computed by adding the two highest response categories for each question (on a 5-point scale).

Conclusion

Until more consumer-relevant outcome measures for care and health plan performance are developed, enrollee satisfaction remains one of the best measures of health plan performance. It has been amply demonstrated that reliable, valid information can be gained from surveys of consumers. Three practical, take-away lessons learned from participation in the Oregon Consumer Scorecard Consortium are as follows:

1. *Surveys must be conducted on an annual basis.* OMAP learned that publishing annual data allows individual managed care plans to make quality improvement efforts and that those improvements can be reflected in consumer satisfaction scores in a timely manner. The presentation of consumer satisfaction data is a powerful market force and should be respected as such. Presenting obsolete survey information can unfairly penalize or reward certain managed care plans and will provide less-than-useful information to information-hungry consumers.

2. *Data must be uniformly collected, consistent in content, and comparably reported.* Survey instrumentation and administration must be consistent across health plans. Surveys should be conducted by an independent research organization not affiliated with any of the managed care plans being analyzed. This independent source should be sufficiently impartial as to not be judged by consumers as holding a particular bias or ax to grind.

3. *Those responsible for survey design must be able to live with the decisions that shaped the final product.* All parties to the process, from the consumer to purchasers to the managed care health plans, will want to track health plan performance over time. Every change made in a survey instrument, the sampling strategy, or survey administration will alter the ability to interpret change over time; therefore, each decision about changes should be made carefully. Scorecards themselves should be subject to a continuous quality

improvement process; therefore, revisions will be necessary to reflect the changing delivery system that is being monitored.

A major challenge that remains in consumer research is that of creating tools that will accurately assess the performance of managed care organizations across Medicaid, Medicare, and commercially insured populations. These finely calibrated tools will be essential to ensuring equity and quality across patient populations, regardless of insurance source. Fortunately, many of the lessons learned from the Oregon project can be applied to other populations, in spite of the fact that the survey instrument was designed for a Medicaid population.

Epilogue

In 1996, the federal Agency for Health Care Policy Research funded a consortium of researchers to develop a standardized consumer satisfaction survey instrument that can be adapted to various patient populations. At the time of this printing, the Consumer Assessment of Health Plans Survey project has released drafts of tailored Medicare and Medicaid instruments. The use of the Medicare instrument will be required by the Health Care Financing Administration—the federal agency with oversight responsibilities for the Medicare and Medicaid programs—of all health plans with a Medicare risk contract.

The CAHPS instruments will offer yet another opportunity for standardizing consumer surveys that can be used in future scorecard efforts. If widely disseminated, CAHPS data could form the basis for comparable data within and between states, regionally and nationally, and thus provide consumers with data that can be benchmarked against best-practice plans and providers. A caveat to the CAHPS instruments is that it has been designed for a broad audience, and their applicability to special populations should be carefully scrutinized. Tailoring scorecards to be responsive to the information needs of the most vulnerable among us will be an important and necessary activity.

References

Aday, L. A. *Designing and Conducting Health Surveys*. San Francisco: Jossey-Bass, 1996.

Babbie, E. *The Practice of Social Research*. (7th ed.) Belmont, Calif.: Wadsworth, 1995.

Baldasare, P. M. "Should Marketers Care About Satisfying Medicaid Patients?" *Journal of Health Care Marketing*, 1995, *32*(2), 32.

Davies, A. R., and Ware, J. E., Jr. *GHAA's Consumer Satisfaction Survey and User's Manual*. Washington, D.C.: American Association of Health Plans (formerly Group Health Association of America), 1991.

Dillman, D. *Mail and Telephone Surveys: The Total Design Method*. New York: Wiley, 1978.

Hall, M. F. "Patient Satisfaction or Acquiescence? Comparing Mail and Telephone Survey Results." *Journal of Health Care Marketing*, 1995, *15*(8), 54.

Hanes, P., and Greenlick, M. *Oregon Consumer Scorecard Project, Final Report*. Publication No. 97-N008, Rockville, Md.: U.S. Department of Health and Human Services, 1996.

Kiefe, C. I., and Hyman, D. J. "Do Public Health Clinic Systems Provide Health Care Access for the Urban Poor? A Cross-sectional Study." *Journal of Community Health*, 1996, *21*, 61–70.

Pascoe, G. C. "Patient Satisfaction in Primary Health Care." *Evaluation and Program Planning*, 1983, *6*, 185–210.

Sudman, S., Finn, A. and Lannom, L. "The Use of Bounded Recall Procedures in Single Interviews." *Public Opinion Quarterly*, 1984, *48*, 520–524.

Ware, J. E., Jr., Snyder, M., Wright, W. R., and Davies, A. R. "Defining Patient Satisfaction with Medical Care." *Evaluation and Program Planning*, 1983, *6*, 247–263.

Ware, J. E., Jr., *SF–36 Health Status Survey*. The Health Institute, New England Medical Center, Boston, 1993.

Chapter Seven

Measuring Health Care Quality

The Process and Outcomes of Care

Bruce W. Goldberg

At a time when consumers are being offered a widening array of choices of health care systems, each organized and delivered quite differently, the industry is lagging seriously behind in its ability to provide information that can help consumers make choices among health plan options. Lacking quality and performance information, consumers often choose a plan based primarily on cost considerations. Although cost is appropriately a major concern, value—purchasing high-quality health care at an affordable price—is an equally important consideration.

Fundamental to determining the value of health care is the ability to define quality, particularly from a consumer perspective. Previous chapters have discussed consumers' perceptions of quality. This chapter will address issues related to the relevance and practicality of providing measures of clinical quality to consumers. The challenges of data specification, measurement, and reporting of quality information will also be discussed.

Measuring and Defining Clinical Quality

Findings from a 1996 national survey cosponsored by the Henry J. Kaiser Family Foundation and the Agency for Health Care Policy and Research (AHCPR) show that 42 percent of Americans interviewed said their most important concern in choosing a health plan was high quality (Princeton Survey Research Associates, 1996). Quality was never defined for respondents of this study, so we are left to impute various meanings to this finding. This is not an easy task because we do not know much about how health care consumers define quality.

Consumer Definitions of Quality

Available research on the subject suggests that individual consumers' views of quality are often different from those of major purchasers, accrediting organizations, and health care professionals. These studies suggest that the important dimensions of quality for consumers are the nature of the physician-patient relationship and the service quality experienced in their physician's office or in a hospital setting. The way accrediting bodies and managed care organizations monitor quality is by measuring administrative structures and policies, by credentialing physicians, and by monitoring population-based performance outcomes. These factors are not particularly relevant to consumers (Hibbard and Jewett, 1997; Princeton Survey Research Associates, 1996).

When respondents in the Kaiser Family Foundation-AHCPR Survey were asked the top factors that influenced them in choosing a doctor, 84 percent stated that how well a doctor communicates with patients and shows a caring attitude would have *a lot of influence*, whereas only 25 percent would be highly influenced by how a doctor had been rated by a government or independent agency.

Measuring the various dimensions of health care has proven to be as difficult as defining its quality. The emerging field of quality measurement is fraught with methodological and practical complexities. Consequently, a variety of measurement approaches are either available now or are being developed.

The delivery of health care has been broadly described as having two essential components: technical and interpersonal. Technical factors include the knowledge, skills, and judgment of trained professionals. Interpersonal attributes are those that function as the vehicle through which technical skills are delivered. It is widely believed that technical success depends in large measure on the interpersonal skills of the practitioner. The overall quality of health care has been categorized into three components—structure, process, and outcome (Donabedian, 1966). This framework reflects the essential elements of care and provides a taxonomy that is useful for conceptualizing and measuring quality of care. As noted by Donabedian, structure is the setting in which care occurs, process is what actually happens in the caregiving encounter (both interpersonal and technical), and outcome is the product of the encounter. Good structure enhances both process and outcome, so this framework is useful for assessing quality in the context of the organizationally based health care that is characteristic of the 1990s.

Structural Measures. Structural measures that describe the practice setting, organizational arrangements, and the credentials of the providers of care are commonly used. Likewise, measures of patient satisfaction are often employed to define quality in various health care contexts. Although each definition can provide meaningful information, and indeed patient satisfaction is a significant outcome of care, all the definitions mentioned provide limited information on the technical aspects of care.

Process Measures. Efforts to measure the technical quality of medical care often focus on the activities in which individual health care providers engage in treating their patients; hence, these measures are referred to as *process* measures. In addressing the technical aspects of health care delivery, process indicators are assumed to measure effectiveness of service delivery and, concurrently, the quality of the care delivered. These indicators include how a particular illness or condition is *managed* (for example, whether glycohemoglobin testing is ordered for diabetics), as well as the extent to which immunizations are provided for two-year-olds. Process measures are increasingly more available and, indeed, offer an easy alternative for providers interested in monitoring and improving their own care delivery systems. However, research has yet to demonstrate a clear or consistent relationship between these commonly used process measures and desired outcomes of care. As a result, the health services research community continues to pursue direct measurement of the outcomes of care in its quest for the ideal quality measure (Siu and others, 1992; Eddy and Billings, 1988).

Outcome Measures. Although measuring the outcomes of care may be preferable to process measures, many factors currently limit the utility of outcomes measures. Obtaining reliable, valid outcomes data requires a significant investment of time and effort to abstract medical records and administrative data systems. Even then, the validity of these data is often suspect.

Take, for example, the outcome of treatment for low back pain. The time period between an initial patient visit for low back pain and when that individual is symptom-free (or able to resume usual activities) could be considered an appropriate outcome measure. But our ability to track such "episodes of illness" is often hampered because complete patient information is not contained in the medical record. For other conditions, it may take very long periods of time to measure treatment outcomes. For example, it requires five to ten years to appropriately monitor the outcomes for most types of cancer.

Several noteworthy projects around the country are developing both process and outcome measures of quality, with the goal of measuring health plan performance. The best known of these is the Health Plan Employer Data and Information Set (HEDIS), developed by a group of interested parties, including the National Committee for Quality Assurance (NCQA). The recent version of HEDIS (2.5) consists of more than sixty measures that assess managed care organizations on the quality of management, finance, utilization of services, member services, access to care, and the quality of care. Nine of these measures assess the clinical quality of care. Only two of the nine clinical measures (rates of low-birth-weight newborns and pediatric asthma admissions rates) are considered outcome measures.

The Foundation for Accountability, a public-private alliance of major purchasers that provides health care coverage to more than eighty million people, is developing a new generation of standardized quality measures to be used by both consumers and volume purchasers. The foundation is seeking to focus the nation's attention on the quality of health care and its systematic measurement. It is developing measures of enrollee health status and satisfaction, as well as the performance of health plans in providing care for commonly occurring medical conditions (Foundation for Accountability, 1995).

Several other projects developing clinical performance measures are worth noting. The Agency for Health Care Policy and Research (AHCPR) contracted with the Center for Health Policy Studies to collect and assess existing clinical performance measures and to devise a typology for analyzing the properties of these measures (Duggar and others, 1995). AHCPR also contracted with the Center for Quality of Care Research and Education at the Harvard School of Public Health to develop the Computerized Needs-Oriented Quality Measurement Evaluation System (CONQUEST 1.0), a tool that permits users to collect and evaluate health care quality measurements that are suited to their needs. CONQUEST 1.0 is available on CD ROM and contains two databases describing clinical quality measures and health care conditions that are linked by codes for ease of usability (Palmer and others, 1996). The Delmarva Foundation for Medical Care has developed a typology of quality of ambulatory care measures for Medicare beneficiaries. Finally, AHCPR has recently funded a five-year project—the Consumers Assessment of Health Plans Survey (CAHPS)—to develop survey instruments for assessing the quality of health care from a consumer perspective (Edgeman-Levitan and Cleary, 1996).

Consumer Interest in Clinical Quality Measures

Whether and how clinical quality measures can be used by consumers has yet to be determined. To date, clinical quality measures have been used primarily by health care organizations in quality improvement efforts and, increasingly, by corporate purchasers of health insurance for negotiating purposes (Leatherman and Chase, 1994). Few of these quality performance measures have been provided to individual consumers for their use in choosing a health plan. A recent report found that of seventy-seven purchasers polled, only four made health plan performance data available to their employees during open enrollment. In each case, the purchaser has only recently provided HEDIS quality indicators to consumers, so no finding of their usefulness or relevance for consumer choice has been established. However, one study that looked at the relevance of HEDIS measures to consumers in a focus group context found that most of the HEDIS measures reviewed were felt to be of marginal utility to the focus group participants (Hibbard and Jewett, 1994).

With regard to clinical quality, consumers' informational needs are extremely diverse, and no measures seem to be of common interest to all. Among all consumers, those with chronic or disabling medical conditions appear to be the most interested in clinical quality information as it relates to the management of their particular condition. As other authors have noted in this volume, consumers are interested in quality information that is relevant to people like themselves (Hanes and Greenlick, 1996; Edgeman-Levitan and Cleary, 1996).

Personalized information reflects where in the life cycle an individual resides. Younger, healthy people may be interested in preventive services; families with young children may be interested in the accessibility of well-child exams; elders with chronic conditions may want to know about condition-specific care management services. Put another way, information regarding glycohemoglobin testing is better understood and of greater utility to a diabetic than to the general population of health plan enrollees. Likewise, information about a plan's childhood immunization practices is of little use to members without children. As would be expected in any market, consumers are far more interested in the quality of care provided by their own physician than in measures of physician performance on a planwide basis. Only to the extent that an individual anticipates the need for specialists or other service their plan has to offer does interest in these performance measures increase.

In addition, participants in the Oregon Consumer Scorecard Project's focus groups noted that they had some difficulty interpreting quality information and felt they did not have the knowledge or expertise to judge clinical competence. So saying, these consumers expressed interest in having access to unbiased, expert opinion about what would constitute clinical quality of care (Hanes and Greenlick, 1996). Finally, when given comparative quality information, consumers were only interested in these data to the extent that they presented real and meaningful differences among plans. We learned from our focus groups that simply presenting comparative data with statistical differences noted, but without references to clinical significance, is more confusing than illuminating to most consumers.

Given the heterogeneity of consumer interest, it is not surprising that clinical quality information presented in a variety of published report cards has been met with mixed feedback (Research Triangle Institute, 1995). What we have not fully explored is whether the information itself or its presentation is of limited utility for consumers. Even the most savvy consumers and health care professionals have difficulty interpreting some technical clinical quality information. Therefore, it remains an untested hypothesis that clinical quality information, presented in an understandable and relevant way, will be of use to consumers for decision-making purposes.

Challenges in Measuring and Reporting Quality

Lack of consensus between and within provider groups and consumers on the most useful indicators of clinical quality makes choosing meaningful quality measures a formidable task for scorecard designers. Consumers want information that is personally and clinically relevant. Collecting this tailored information can be difficult because of the small numbers involved, and it can be costly.

Alternatively, a one-size-fits-all approach to presenting clinical quality information will certainly lack relevance to most consumers.

Among health professionals, the preferred criteria applied to the development of clinical quality measures are (1) a focus on conditions that occur frequently or are associated with a high cost or unfavorable outcome, (2) measurement of factors with the potential to change provider behavior and thus improve patient outcomes, (3) inclusion of data that are readily available, serve some educational purpose, can be linked to public health objectives, and can be compared across plans, and (4) inclusion of data when sufficient clinical agreement exists as to how best to treat the condition. However, there is little agreement among health professionals about which data to collect—which conditions or clinical measures to evaluate—to ensure that health plans are providing quality medical care.

Unit of Analysis

The level at which clinical quality data are analyzed and compared is of critical importance. To date, only data at the individual health plan level have been analyzed and reported. Comparing quality data between two plans, if each had their own exclusive provider panels, could provide meaningful comparisons. However, in most health care markets, individual providers contract with many different plans. Therefore, comparing data among plans with overlapping provider panels may not provide consumers with useful information because it isn't possible to differentiate plan from provider effects. Complicating matters even further is the fact that most consumers have expressed an interest in information about individual providers, not about health plans.

Uniformity and Comparability of Data

If clinical quality information is to be useful in helping consumers choose a health plan, it must be comparable across all plans. Comparability requires standardized indicators, data collection methods, analysis, and reporting. Measuring childhood immunization rates provides a good example of some of the difficulties that may be encountered, even in situations that appear simple and straight-forward.

As noted in a report issued by the General Accounting Office (GAO), one plan may report the number of children between birth and two years of age who received at least four diphtheria-pertussis-tetanus immunizations, whereas another may report the number of children between the ages of twelve months and two years who received at least three shots. Further, one plan may use as its denominator all children who were members during the reporting period, whereas another may use a sample of members who had been continuously enrolled for two years and who had used health services at least once (General Accounting Office, 1994). For these data to be comparable, identical specifications for obtaining numerators and denominators must be used.

Reporting to Consumers

Reporting of information must be done so it is meaningful to con-sumers; charts, graphs, and labels must be understandable. More important, consumers need to be provided with a clear explanation of what each clinical measure means, as well as the reason for its inclusion on a scorecard. The Xerox HMO Performance Report is unique in this regard, as it explicitly states the goal for each mea-sure included. Consumers are therefore able to judge how well each plan is performing compared to a set of absolute benchmarks, as well as to other plans (Hoy, Wicks, and Forland, 1996). Providing information that is understandable and meaningful to the typical consumer requires not only effort and creativity in the production of such information but also requires continuous evaluation of the utility of such information.

As noted earlier, consumers are not interested in clinical qual-ity information unless a scorecard presents real and meaningful differences. The issue of *meaningful differences* is most complex. Does meaningful difference suggest that only statistically significant information be presented to consumers? What about the issue of clinical significance?

When large samples are used, relatively small differences can be statistically significant. For example, two health plans might have childhood immunization rates of 95 percent and 91 percent. The rates may represent a statistically significant difference, but to most professionals and consumers alike, they do not represent a clinically meaningful difference in the performance of the two plans. Conversely, some reporting models might report large differences that are not significant, yet each measure is the best point estimate of the plan's performance. How this information is presented and explained to consumers is critical. But simply presenting comparative health plan differences that are not meaningful creates confusion, can give a false sense of difference, and can ultimately penalize or reward a health plan inappropriately.

Risk Adjustment

Experience has shown that reporting clinical performance without appropriate severity or risk adjustment can result in misinformation and could work against the goal of providing consumers with useful and reliable information on which to judge health care performance. (For a fuller discussion of this point see Chapter One.)

Denominator Issues

Providing consumers with comparable data requires that the denominator of a measure be calculated uniformly across plans. In order to do so, two issues must be addressed. First, the population of managed care organizations is constantly changing; members are continuously enrolling and disenrolling. Without adjusting for this fluctuation, comparison across organizations with differing enrollment and disenrollment rates could be misleading. Second, even when enrollment and disenrollment rates are controlled, characteristics of members may differ greatly across plans. Plan memberships may differ not only in the severity of illness (that is, case mix) but also in demographic and sociocultural factors, which can each affect care-seeking behavior and outcomes.

Even when denominators are comparable, they may not be large enough to calculate reliable rates for certain condition-specific indicators or within certain population groups. This is a particular problem with Medicaid populations. Because of eligibility requirements, recipients move on and off public assistance frequently. As a result, the enrollment-disenrollment turnover is generally higher in a Medicaid population than among commercially insured populations.

Pilot-Testing Medicaid HEDIS

The experience of two health plans participating in the Oregon Consumer Scorecard Project provides a graphic illustration of the many challenges that scorecard developers will encounter in collecting and reporting health plan performance measures. A specific activity undertaken in conjunction with developing the scorecard prototype was to pilot-test the collection of three Medicaid HEDIS measures: prenatal care utilization, well-child examinations in the first year of life, and glycohemoglobin testing among diabetics. These measures were selected because of their high prevalence in the population and because of their potential educational and community health improvement value. The two health plans agreeing to collect the data at the time of the Medicaid HEDIS exercise each had more than twenty thousand OHP-Medicaid members.

In completing the glycohemoglobin-monitoring measure, only one plan could identify a denominator of as many as sixty-seven diabetics who fit the measure's specifications, that is, diabetics enrolled in the health plan for at least one year (allowing for only a one-month break in enrollment).

For the well-child measure, another plan noted:

We thought we had sufficient sample size to complete the well-child measure but this turns out not to be the case. We found about 1,100 children whose 15–month birthday occurred during 1995, but when we applied the measure's eligibility criteria, that is, continuous enrollment from 31 days of life and no breaks in service, the eligible population dropped to about 100 infants. Allowing for a single month break in eligibility raised the eligible population to about 300 infants. Given that, the sample size is not adequate following the measure specifications, and that the specs do not provide offsets in the event of breaks in eligibility, we will not be able to complete this measure [Hanes and Greenlick, 1996].

Data Collection Issues

The three major sources of data from which clinical quality information can be obtained include a plan's administrative data, medical record reviews, and direct member surveys. Abstracting information from medical records is generally the most expensive and time consuming of these methods. Using administrative data presents a variety of standardization of information issues; foremost is the fact that plans collect information in noncomparable ways. A direct patient survey may be the most reliable means of estimating certain clinical outcomes. However, case-finding can be difficult, and this can be an expensive and labor-intensive process.

Because it is relatively easy and less expensive, health plans prefer to use the administrative data contained in claims, clinical encounters, membership, billing, and pharmacy databases to obtain clinical quality information whenever possible. However, many plans in Oregon expressed concern about the reliability and validity of their administrative data systems for this purpose (Hanes and Greenlick, 1996).

Data collection and reporting for quality monitoring purposes among health plans is very much in its infancy. Existing health plan administrative data sets are designed for uses other than monitoring clinical quality information. Consequently, their ability to reliably capture the content and quality of a clinical encounter is extremely limited. Encounter or billing data are currently the source of the majority of clinical quality information. However, a variety of problems exist within these systems, which include the following:

Coding is not uniform. Health care providers and their office staff often will code incorrectly or inconsistently, thereby compromising the validity of the data.

Multiple services are provided during a single encounter, but only one is captured. Many services may be provided during a single office visit but not captured in the administrative data. For example, a child's visit for an upper-respiratory infection (URI) might be used as an opportunity to conduct a well-child screen. If the visit is coded solely as URI, the well-child examination is not captured.

Administrative data do not capture needed information. In a variety of situations, administrative data do not capture the information needed to calculate rates for a measure. For example, diabetic foot exams are not generally coded in administrative data sets. Therefore, this type of information would need to be generated from a medical record review.

Data sets are not integrated at the plan level. Within health plans, different data sets, such as pharmacy and clinical encounter data, may not be set up to communicate with each other. Among plans, similar data sets may not even be available. For example, some staff and group model HMOs do not use billing data and therefore rely solely on an appointment system for their encounter data. Such data systems do not articulate with the billing and encounter systems used by other plans.

Medical record review may be a more effective way to collect clinical quality information, but it is also significantly more costly. Substantial time is needed from a nurse or medical records technician trained in abstracting medical information directly from a patient's record. The relative quality and comprehensiveness of medical record reviews can differ significantly with the skill of the reviewer. In addition, because different individuals abstract data, achieving uniformity in data collection is not possible. Likewise, there is little standardization in how patient encounter information is recorded by health care providers, so the content of a visit can be described differently by different providers, and important clinical information can be missed.

Resource Utilization

The resources needed to obtain clinical quality information are not well documented, particularly for administrative data. Costs will vary depending on the method used. There is general consensus that medical record review is most costly. However, costs for administrative data collection vary greatly, depending on the sophistication of the information systems available. The DEMPAQ study found that medical record reviewers averaged just under an hour per medical record to abstract data for up to 256 indicators per case. In addition, fifteen to thirty minutes per record was the time reported for other review-related activities. The cost averaged $49 per record—ranging between $35 and $73—depending on the state where the review was conducted (Duggar and Palmer, 1995). Another study involving 37,000 hospital medical records found that abstracting and coding hospital charts took fifteen to thirty minutes per record, quality control averaged ten minutes per record, and clerical support time averaged fifteen minutes per record. The total direct and indirect costs were $40 per record in 1993 dollars (Center for Health Policy Studies, 1995).

How Quality Information Can Be Used

One of the unresolved issues surrounding clinical quality information is its intended purpose. It can be used to help consumers choose health plans and providers. It can also be used for continuous quality improvement within health plans, used as an educa-tional tool for consumers, or used as a regulatory tool. Each is a potentially laudable and worthwhile function.

Currently, because of the collection and reporting challenges just noted, quality information has been of little use to consumers as they try to make choices. There are several reasons for this, including, consumers' lack of understanding of the technical aspects of quality, the questionable utility of indicators selected, the way quality information is presented, and simply because consumer interest in the technical quality of care for choice decisions is not well understood. Even less is known about the usefulness of quality information as an educational tool.

Some postulate that quality information can, in fact, be a powerful educational tool. As consumers become more sophisti-cated about the technical aspects and outcomes of care, they may begin to pressure the industry into greater accountability in these areas. Currently, consumers are most sensitive to cost. Although personal finances dictate much of this focus, lower cost is a factor that most consumers have come to understand and bargain for accordingly. However, quality is poorly understood. In a market-place where consumers are expected to compare cost and quality, that is, to seek value, they are currently operating at a distinct dis-advantage.

There is a role for easily understood clinical quality information in educating consumers about its importance for a variety of rea-sons. For example, presenting quality information about a health plan's performance at getting women over the age of fifty years to have a mammogram is providing education about the basic epi-demiology of breast cancer, including the purposes and importance of mammography in early breast cancer detection.

Although rarely used as such, there may also be an important role for clinical quality information as a regulatory tool. Currently, most state insurance regulatory agencies monitor the administra-tive and fiscal practices of the health insurance industry but not the outcomes associated with the consumption of their products.

Regulation ensures that health insurers have adequate financial reserves to pay claims, that premiums and benefits are fairly distributed, and that consumers' rights are protected, but insurance commissioners have rarely examined clinical quality and held plans accountable for providing quality service. State medical licensing boards have paid some attention to clinical quality as they have monitored the individual professional practice of medicine. As information regarding individual physicians' clinical quality becomes more available, the extent to which medical boards will use this information remains to be seen. Real and meaningful quality feedback loops that extend from consumers to health plans to states and medical boards and back to consumers would be a laudable public policy function.

Regardless of the purpose of reporting quality information, the issue of consumer participation is critical. Consumer involvement in the choice of quality indicators is critical. The quality indicators chosen for public scrutiny will surely have significant resources and attention directed at them. Given their potential importance in the medical marketplace, the question of who defines quality remains: Will consumers dictate what information is reported on health plan scorecards and other choice tools, or will professionals determine their content? To date, HEDIS and other comparable measures have largely been developed by health professionals, industry leaders, and major purchasers of care.

Getting to Accountability and Value

As noted earlier, existing population-based performance measures have minimal relevance to most consumers, yet their potential to shape the quality of care and hold health plans accountable is great. HEDIS is now widely used, yet it remains of questionable value to consumers. Will it be possible to modify HEDIS to make it more relevant to consumers, or will new measurement tools and reporting systems need to be developed? Modifying HEDIS will require a greater understanding of consumer information needs and meaningful participation of consumers in the modification process.

The resources required to collect and present quality information are substantial. Currently, health plans are producing clinical performance data for a variety of audiences, including the National Committee for Quality Assurance for accreditation, state professional review organizations, internal quality improvement activities, and purchaser requirements (both public and private). Most of these competing, data-driven activities use distinctly different data specifications. Consolidating quality reporting, while at the same time allowing for meaningful consumer participation and input, is critical. The challenge that remains in health plan performance reporting is how to deal with the conflicting notions of quality held by consumers, group purchasers, and health professionals.

References

Center for Health Policy Studies. *Final Report: Study to Investigate the Accuracy and Completeness with Which Medicare Claims Data Summarize the Medical Record*. Agency for Health Care Policy and Research, Contract No. 282–91–0073, Rockville, Md., 1995.

Donabedian, A. "Evaluating the Quality of Medical Care." *Milbank Quarterly*, 1966, *44*, 166–203.

Duggar, B., and others. *Understanding and Choosing Clinical Performance Measures for Quality Improvement: Development of a Typology*. Agency for Health Care Policy and Research, Contract No. 95-N001, Mar. 1995.

Duggar, B., and Palmer, R. H. *Final Report: Understanding and Choosing Clinical Performance Measures for Quality Improvement: Development of a Typology*. Agency for Health Care Policy and Research, Contract No. 282–92–0038, Jan. 1995.

Eddy, D. M., and Billings, J. "The Quality of Medical Evidence: Implications for Quality of Care." *Health Affairs*, 1988, *7*(1), 19–32.

Edgeman-Levitan, S., and Cleary, P. "What Information Do Consumers Want and Need?" *Health Affairs*, 1996, *15*(4), 42–56.

Foundation for Accountability. *Guidebook for Performance Measurement*. Portland, Oreg., 1995.

General Accounting Office. *Health Care Reform: Report Cards Are Useful, but Significant Issues Need to Be Addressed*. Report to the Chairman, Committee on Labor and Human Resources, U.S. Senate, General Accounting

Office/Health, Education and Human Services Division HEHS-94-219. Washington, D.C., 1994.

Hanes, P., and Greenlick, M. *Oregon Consumer Scorecard Project Final Report.* Agency for Health Care Policy and Research Publication No. 97-N008, Rockville, Md.: U.S. Department of Health and Human Services, 1996.

Hibbard, J. H., and Jewett, J. J. *Preliminary Findings from Consumers Comprehension of Quality of Care Indicators.* Agency for Health Care Policy and Research, Contract R01-08231, 1994.

Hibbard J. H., and Jewett J. J. "Will Quality Report Cards Help Consumers?" *Health Affairs,* 1997, *16*(3), 218–228.

Hoy, E. W., Wicks, E. K., and Forland, R. A. "A Guide to Facilitating Consumer Choice." *Health Affairs,* 1996, *15*(4), 9–30.

Leatherman, S., and Chase, D. "Using Report Cards to Grade Health Plan Quality." *Journal of American Health Policy,* Jan./Feb. 1994, pp. 32–40.

Palmer, H., and others. *CONQUEST 1.0: Overview of Final Report and User's Guide.* Agency for Health Care Policy and Research, Publication No. 96-N009, Apr. 1996.

Princeton Survey Research Associates. "Americans as Health Care Consumers: The Role of Quality Information." A survey commissioned by the Kaiser Family Foundation and the Agency for Health Care Policy and Research, Oct. 1996.

Research Triangle Institute. "Design of a Survey to Monitor Consumers' Access to Care, Uses of Health Services, Health Outcomes, and Patient Satisfaction." Final Report to the Health Care Financing Administration, Contract No. 500-94-0048, Mar. 1995.

Siu, A. L., and others. "Choosing Quality of Care Measures Based on the Expected Impact of Improved Care on Health." *Health Services Research,* 1992, *27*(5), 619–650.

Chapter Eight

The Alchemy of Accountability

Science and Art of Consumer Scorecards

Pamela P. Hanes and Merwyn R. Greenlick

The Oregon Consumer Scorecard Consortium was formed to test the feasibility of collecting, interpreting, and publishing health plan performance information of interest to Oregon consumers. Specifically, consortium members and staff sought to test the feasibility of reporting comparative health plan information by geographic area, while recognizing the unique information needs of consumers with special health care needs.

This reporting of comparative consumer satisfaction data and population-based health plan performance measures was intended to be responsive to the expressed information preferences of individual consumers, both in terms of content and format. Included among the goals of the prototype development process was that of learning how to translate expert judgments of quality into consumer-relevant information and to assess the resources needed for accomplishing this goal.

The consortium came to appreciate that scorecard utility was a multidimensional concept. A scorecard would be judged by its usefulness to consumers as they make choices among health care plans, as well as its ability to achieve the broader social goal of improving quality and value in health services delivery.

Lessons Learned

The sections to follow summarize the many lessons learned as we pursued our goal, which was *to develop an analytically and conceptually sound scorecard that incorporates a broad range of perspectives and expertise, including consumers, health services researchers, clinicians, health plan representatives, and state-level policymakers.*

Meaningful Presentation of Differences

A major challenge in scorecard development was to present comparative health plan data, both for satisfaction and performance, that was meaningful, understandable, reliable, and of use to consumers. The popular media frequently critique managed health care and capitated forms of health care reimbursement. The resulting public mood is one of heightened interest in the subject but sparse objective information on which to judge the adequacy of the health care options that consumers face in the marketplace. This politically charged environment created a special challenge for the consortium as we attempted to produce comparative information that could stand up to the scrutiny and rigor of legitimate research and analytical methods and have the confidence of its end users—consumers.

Consumers and health plans alike expressed a powerful message that a scorecard should only present *real and meaningful* differences among health plans. Health plan representatives and consumers involved in the consortium's activities noted that scorecards could report health plan performance ratings that were statistically significant in their differences but not clinically meaningful. Numerous examples of such confusing messages were highlighted during our data collection, analysis, and reporting activities. Reporting difference was not a trivial matter. It was intellectually humbling to the academic partners to acknowledge that statistics don't tell the whole story in many measurement situations.

An alternative measurement scenario is instructive here. Several health plans with a statewide market area had statistically different member satisfaction ratings between their rural and urban plan members. Although the differences were relatively small because scores were based on statewide averages, the numbers made the difference between a plan receiving an average, above average, or below average rating compared to the average of all health plans. In fairness to those plans that had competitive satisfaction ratings in their urban markets, scores needed to be reported on a rural-urban basis. It was important to recognize that many rural primary care provider networks are lean, providing minimal-to-no choice for health plan contracting and consumer choice purposes. This situation graphically demonstrated that a small group of physicians with unhappy patients had the potential to pull satisfaction scores down for an entire health plan, particularly for small plans operating in rural markets. This was an important lesson.

This rural health resource dilemma raised interesting public policy questions, particularly as scorecard issues intersect with rural workforce development and health providers' continuing education policies. Because one potential function of a consumer scorecard should be to monitor health plan performance and feed this performance data back to health plans for quality improvement purposes, how primary care access, availability, and quality of care issues are managed is highly significant to scorecard developers.

Differences in Perceptions of Quality

As discussed in previous chapters, population-based performance measures reportedly have minimal relevance to most consumers, yet their potential to shape quality of care and hold health plans accountable is great. This is particularly true in areas of quality monitoring where measures have yet to be developed, for example, managing secondary conditions among persons with disabilities, monitoring the outcomes of cancer treatment over time, and formulating growth and development indicators for children in managed care plans. Finding the balance between expert judgments of health plan performance that are based on reliable clinical standards and individual consumers' notions of quality will continue to challenge scorecard development efforts.

Use of HEDIS Measures

The consortium learned that the ability to collect and report Medicaid HEDIS measures was limited by the on-again, off-again enrollment patterns of the Medicaid population. This discontinuity in enrollment worked against using HEDIS measures as they were currently specified.

Health plan performance monitoring is an area of public policy where many positive interventions are possible. Performance monitoring may well lead to a reappraisal of the current eligibility requirements found in the Medicaid program that work against improving the health and well-being of vulnerable populations.

A further challenge of HEDIS is its dubious value to consumers. Scorecard developers may want to test new ways to collect and report population-based measures. For example, they might want to look for measures other than HEDIS measures that more closely reflect the health status of a scorecard's target population. Just as the consortium looked at morbidity and mortality statistics and adult risk behavior data in Oregon, scorecard developers are advised to look to population-based benchmarks that could serve as an accountability grounding for specific populations.

The obvious drawback to this approach is data burden, especially given the data requirements already imposed on health plans for NCQA accreditation. On this point, a consortium approach can be most useful because it provides a vehicle for collaboration among purchasers, insurers, and providers. That allows for managing the data collection burden and negotiating it in the most appropriate and efficient way to meet the needs of all stakeholders involved, including the population served.

Consumers want more accountability from health plans and from those who purchase health care on their behalf. Further, they want to be confident in the reliability and uniformity of the quality information that is provided. Consumers are savvy about what constitutes marketing hype and expect something different from a scorecard. A real and meaningful quality feedback loop that extends from the state to health plans and providers to consumers and back to the state should be a top public policy goal of consumer scorecard efforts.

Tailoring of Information

Consumers express a strong preference for choice information that is personally relevant. Equally significant, comparative information ought to be geographically sensitive. Rural consumers want to know about the performance of plans doing business in their area, even if the choice is limited. A one-size-fits-all scorecard may be the most practical approach, but it will ultimately not be relevant to consumers who aren't that one size. Population differences require sensitivity to geographic factors, health plan market areas, health status, and so forth. This tailoring issue will challenge the development and reporting of both satisfaction and health plan performance measures in the future as health plans, survey researchers, and scorecard developers search for the illusive population denominator.

Functions of a Consumer Scorecard

Although it is reasonable to assume that a health plan scorecard can fulfill many functions, from reporting comparable information to educating consumers about how to be more prudent purchasers and monitor quality, scorecard development is politically and methodologically complex and should proceed with modest goals.

It may be necessary to evaluate the preferred functions of a scorecard relative to other methods of providing consumers with health plan and provider information. Consumers have expressed a powerful need for objective information on which to base health plan choice, judge the quality of care they receive, and better understand how to navigate within complex managed care organizations.

For example, consumers have told us the importance of finding a plan in which their preferred primary care provider practices.

Currently, our ability to provide up-to-date information about provider-plan affiliations, including whether providers are accepting new patients, is very limited. Making physician and other primary care provider information readily available should be a high priority for purchasers, policymakers, and consumer scorecard developers. Realistically, a scorecard may not be the vehicle for disseminating this volatile information. The costs and benefits of various presentation modes must be evaluated and more precisely tailored messages sent to their preferred medium.

Costs of Scorecard Production

Currently, health plans are producing clinical performance data for a variety of audiences, including NCQA for accreditation, the state Professional Review Organization (PRO) for quality reviews, internal quality improvement activities, and myriad individual purchasers' requirements (both public and private). Requests for data and quality monitoring will only increase as time passes and the ability to measure outcomes increases. At the present time, most of these competing data requests use distinctly different data specifications. A key objective of the Oregon consortium was to consolidate and reduce the data burden on health plans through the development of uniform data specifications and sharing of health care information. This objective has not been achieved, although recent legislation passed in Oregon (see Chapter One) will greatly facilitate this consolidation function.

The costs of producing a consumer-friendly scorecard that is reliable, valid, and understandable to consumers will need to be borne by both public and private interests; therefore, these costs must be justifiable in both the short and long run. Costs of production will be affected by the content and media through which the scorecard information is delivered to consumers. As scorecards are being developed, it is recommended that a resource assessment be included in the work plan. As Oregon and other states and principalities move forward with scorecard development, the field will be much better informed about the cost-effectiveness and utility of scorecards as choice and continuous quality improvement tools in the health care sector.

The cost of producing the scorecard prototype in Oregon was relatively minor and was spread over a two-year period. The consortium was able to leverage a $200,000 contract with in-kind contributions from state agencies and fourteen different health plans. It would be difficult to estimate the hours and dollars involved, but if the effort had been fully funded, it is clear that the costs would have been substantial.

Risk-Adjustment of Performance Measures

It has been well established in the literature that patient characteristics contribute to the overall cost and use of health services (Joung, van der Meer, and Mackenbach, 1995; Billi and others, 1993; Stuart and Steinwachs, 1993; Wagner and Hendrich, 1993). Also, satisfied patients are more active partners in their care and treatment regimens, which generally results in better outcomes. In short, the relationship between patient satisfaction and outcomes of care is a robust one, both from a cost and a quality perspective. Because patient characteristics influence many dimensions of the health care experience, it is important to consider their addition to the satisfaction equation as they may serve as a needed moderating factor in risk-adjusting member satisfaction scores.

A first step in deciding whether to adjust satisfaction ratings based on member characteristics is to assess whether the identified characteristics are disproportionately distributed among health plans and thus skewing scores. For example, in Oregon we analyzed a range of demographic characteristics (age, gender, health status, place of residence, and length of time on plan) among the 1996 OHP Satisfaction Survey respondents and found these population characteristics to be evenly distributed across all health plans.

Therefore, we did not need to risk-adjust health plan scores. It was highly possible that this could have turned out differently, with one or more health plans having a disproportionate share of older patients or persons with chronic health conditions. In this event, risk adjustment of the scores would have been an appropriate and necessary function.

Voluntary Versus Regulatory Approaches

A powerful lesson learned in Oregon was that much could be accomplished in the production of a consumer scorecard through a voluntary partnership effort. One significant caveat to voluntary efforts is that individual health plans must all agree that timely and uniform data collection is a high priority. This was not always the case in our prototype development activities, as internal organizational priorities often took precedence over the consortium's time frame. A committed statewide effort to produce a reliable and uniform consumer scorecard would require voluntary, committed participation from high levels in each health plan's organization.

The limited Medicaid HEDIS pilot demonstrated that collecting from one to three measures required giving the participating health plans four months' lead time to collect and report the measure on a voluntary basis. If Oregon were to move to a single consumer satisfaction instrument for both Medicaid and commercially insured consumers, it could well require a mandate to achieve the needed compliance of all affected constituencies.

It is probably not possible, at present, to produce uniform survey instruments and uniform health plan and provider performance standards and data specifications by which all health plans, providers, and purchasers agree to comply. Adding further complexity is that any standards or measures of accountability must be independently audited on a periodic basis to ensure continuing conformance with the specifications and procedures. This auditing function is not inexpensive.

Production of a Consumer Scorecard

Given the political nature of public reporting of comparative health plan information and the potential economic consequences involved, it is of critical importance to have an objective third party responsible for the production of scorecards. This third party should have the trust and confidence of all vested interests and include the necessary technical expertise to collect, analyze, and produce comparative information, as well as be willing to serve as an information clearinghouse and mediator among all interests involved.

The Alchemy of Accountability

As noted in Chapter Two, the story of the Oregon Consumer Scorecard Consortium is one told through the voices and experiences of a voluntary consortium of public and private stakeholders in Oregon. The voices we most wanted to hear were those of consumers. We conclude this volume with some of the more important messages they sent our way.

Choice and voice. The most appropriate and worthwhile function of a consumer scorecard is to support the autonomy and self-determination of individual consumers in making choices among health plans. Additionally, a scorecard should be a means for improving the quality and responsiveness of health plans to consumer concerns.

No hype, please. The idea of a scorecard only makes sense where there are real choices. This is especially true when factoring in geographic, social, cultural, or other special needs considerations.

Human contact. Getting information from an inanimate source has serious limitations, even from an interactive source such as a computer kiosk. A scorecard needs to be backed up by an advice counselor, telephone access, or some other mechanism that links health plan shoppers to a live person.

First-order preferences. Specific information to be included on a consumer scorecard should be organized hierarchically; that is, starting with the first-order need to know which physicians belong to what plans, mining down and through to the differences in how health plans manage condition-specific illness episodes or continuity of care.

Information we can understand. Information about the technical quality of health care is critically important, but most consumers do not currently feel competent to judge clinical quality. Until this information can be made understandable and widely available, consumers' satisfaction ratings of their experience of health care can most appropriately serve as a proxy for technical quality measurement.

People like me. Comparative information about how members evaluate their health plan and its affiliated providers is very important, but these ratings must reflect real differences and be reported in ways that reflect individuals in similar life circumstances. The concept of individualized information preferences was continually reinforced, a poignant reminder of the challenges involved in developing a scorecard that has both individual relevance and broad-based application.

A Final Thought

It is hard to summarize the many lessons learned from Oregon's journey. As much as some consortium members wanted to believe that a consumer-oriented scorecard might be a panacea for choice information, several of us have lingering concerns about its ultimate utility and cost-effectiveness, particularly given the competing interests and priorities of policymakers, purchasers, and health plans. For the consumer scorecard movement to progress as originally conceived, it will require the fiscal and philosophical support of all vested interests on behalf of the goal of informed, value-conscious consumers.

We also have concern about the concepts of voluntariness and consumer purchasing power, as well as about correcting the asymmetry of information that currently exists in the health care marketplace. As these final sentences were being written, the Oregon consortium steering committee was being reconstituted and renamed, with major private and public purchasers being added to its governance structure. The original vision of a consumer-oriented scorecard is being replaced by what some would call a more practical goal. Given the significant costs and effort involved, the Oregon scorecard currently under development will be targeted first at volume purchasers, then at individual consumers. The one lone consumer on the new governing structure will have to shout loudly to make her voice heard. Let's wish her luck.

References

Billi, J. E., and others. "Selection in a Preferred Provider Organization." *Health Services Research*, 1993, 28(5), 563–575.

Joung, I. M., van der Meer, J. B., and Mackenbach, J. P. "Marital Status and Health Care Utilization." *International Journal of Epidemiology*, 1995, 24(3), 569–575.

Stuart, M. E., and Steinwachs, D. M. "Patient-Mix Differences Among Ambulatory Providers and Their Effects on Utilization and Payments to Maryland Medicaid Users." *Medical Care*, 1993, 31(12), 1119–1137.

Wagner, P. J., and Hendrich, J. E. "Physician Views on Frequent Medical Use: Patient Beliefs and Demographic and Diagnostic Correlates." *Journal of Family Practice*, 1993, 36(4), 417–422.

Appendix A

A Consumer Guide to
Selecting a Health Plan

Contents of This Guide

About This Consumer Guide

The Oregon Health Plan is designed to provide the health care you need. To receive services you must choose a health plan from those available in your area.

This guide, also called a "consumer scorecard," provides you with information to compare health plans on the basis of their service, quality, and convenience.

Choosing a health plan is an important decision. This guide is meant to help you make the best choice for you and your family.

Even though all health care is coordinated and delivered through health plans which are required to provide the same basic benefits, there are differences in the way the plans are organized, how services are delivered, what members think about the plan, and how plans do on quality measures.

Several different types of information are included in this guide, and these are described on the next page:

- Benefits/Managed Care
- Doctors/Hospitals
- Service Features
- Member Satisfaction
- Quality Measures
- Health Topics

If you have any questions or would like help using this guide call the toll free number listed below:

1 (800) 297-1234

Managed Care: How Health Plans Provide Care

The Oregon Health Plan uses a system of managed care to provide health services. Under managed care, doctors, hospitals, and other medical professionals partner with an insuring organization to form a **health plan.**

Health plans work at keeping their members healthy by emphasizing **preventive care** and **coordination of care.** Preventive care includes routine examinations, health education, and early detection and treatment of illness.

Your health plan will be responsible for your health care. With most plans, you choose a **primary care provider** (a doctor, nurse or physician assistant) who will coordinate all of your medical care. To receive benefits you must use only the doctors and hospitals affiliated with the health plan you choose, unless otherwise specified. If your primary care provider thinks you need to see a specialist or to be hospitalized, he or she will make such a referral.

If you have special health needs resulting from a chronic health condition or disability, the plan may assign someone to coordinate your care. These professionals are called **care or case managers.**

Urgent care is care available when you have an illness that requires immediate attention. Each plan makes specific arrangements for unscheduled and after-hours care.

Emergency care is available when you have a condition, illness, or injury that is either life-threatening or a serious threat to your health. When such a situation arises, you should go only to the plan's designated emergency rooms.

Standard Benefits: Where the Plans Are the Same

The Oregon Health Plan works hard to keep you healthy by providing many services. All the health plans available to you offer the same standard benefits and are responsible for coordinating these benefits.

What all plans cover:

Diagnosis (tests and exams)

Office visits to doctors or nurses
(including phone consults)

Immunizations (shots)

Check-ups (medical and dental)

Family planning services

Prenatal (maternity) and newborn care

Prescriptions

Hospital services

End-of-life comfort care

Dental services

Alcohol and drug treatment

What is NOT covered:

Conditions which get better on their own, like colds

Experimental treatments

Cosmetic surgery

Most services to help you get pregnant

Pain clinics

Weight loss programs

Doctor Information: Is Your Doctor in the Health Plan?

Not all doctors practice in all plans.

If you have a particular doctor you would like to use, call this toll-free number 1–800–297–1234 to find out:

→ What plan(s) is my doctor in?

or

→ Information about doctors participating in the Oregon Health Plan:

- Specialty
- Age
- Gender
- Hospitals they use
- Clinic Locations / Phone Number
- Office Hours
- Languages Spoken

or

→ Is the doctor I would like to see accepting new patients?

	Medica Value	Healthbest Northwest	Wellness Plus	America Health	First Health	Prime Plan
Doctor in Plan?						

Hospital Location: Where Are the Hospitals in Each Plan?

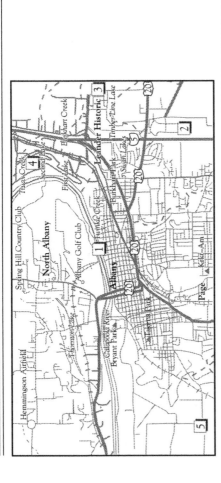

Hospitals

1 Sacred Heart
2 Albany General
3 Lebanon Community
4 Good Samaritan
5 Silverton Community

Hospitals Affiliated with Health Plans	Medica Value	Healthbest Northwest	Wellness Plus	America Health	First Health	Prime Plan
	Sacred Heart	Good Samaritan	Good Samaritan	Silverton Community	Good Samaritan	Good Samaritan
	Salem Memorial	Albany General	Albany General	Salem Memorial	Albany General	Albany General
	Lebanon Community	Lebanon Community	Lebanon Community			

Service Features: Where the Plans Differ

This table shows service features available beyond basic benefits; the information was provided by the health plans in response to a 1996 survey.

	Medica Value	Healthbest Northwest	Wellness Plus	America Health	First Health	Prime Plan
Member Communication						
New Member Orientation (in person)		A		A		
Wellness Newsletter		A		A		
Member Advisory Council*			A	A		
Access to Services						
24-Hour Advice Line (with a live person)	A	A		A	A	
Prescriptions at Retail Stores		A	A	A	A	A
Urgent Care Clinics	A	A		A		A

A = Service Available
Blank = Service Not Available

*A representative group of members who meet to advise the plan about member issues such as access to care, cultural sensitivity and educational materials.

Service Features: Where the Plans Differ, Continued

	Medica Value	Healthbest Northwest	Wellness Plus	America Health	First Health	Prime Plan
Coverage of Non-Physicians						
Chiropractors		Y	Y	Y	Y	
Naturopaths			Y			Y
Acupuncturists			Y			
Massage Therapists			Y			
Access to Specialist & Non-Physicians						
Primary care physician must refer	Y*	Y	Y*	Y		Y
Plan must approve		Y			Y	Y
Self-referrals allowed	Y*		Y*			
Quality Assurance						
Financial rewards given to doctor for:						
increases in patient satisfaction	Y		Y			
decreases in patient complaints	Y					
improving quality of care	Y		Y		Y	

Y = Yes   Blank = No

*For certain services (for example, mental health, chemical dependency and family planning) plan members may self-refer. See plan literature for details about self-referral.

Satisfaction: An Overview of Member Ratings

These ratings are based on the percent (%) of plan members who rated their health plan "very good" or "excellent" and "easy" or "very easy" in response to the questions listed. *For example, significantly more members in Medica Value rated their health plan overall "very good" or "excellent."*

	Medica Value	Healthbest Northwest	Wellness Plus	America Health	First Health	Prime Plan
The Plans How do members rate their health plan overall?	Above Average	Average	Average	Below Average	Average	Average
Doctors and Nurses How satisfied are members with the physicians and nurses in this plan?	Average	Average	Average	Average	Average	Average
Access to Care How easy is it to get medical care in this plan?	Above Average	Average	Average	Below Average	Average	Average
Information How easy is it to get information from the plan?	Average	Average	Average	Below Average	Average	Average

Source: 1996 Oregon Health Plan Consumer Satisfaction Survey

A graph of each question above is on the following page. Member ratings for the entire survey are on pages 11 and 12.

Legend: ○ Below Average   ◐ Average   ● Above Average

Satisfaction: Graphs of Member Ratings

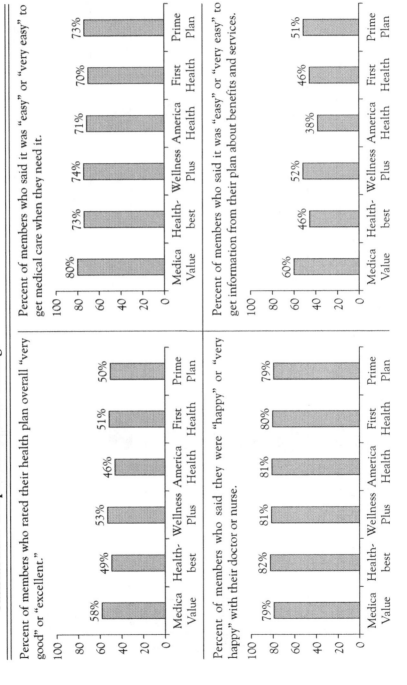

Percent of members who rated their health plan overall "very good" or "excellent."

58%	49%	53%	46%	51%	50%
Medica Value	Health-best	Wellness Plus	America Health	First Health	Prime Plan

Percent of members who said they were "happy" or "very happy" with their doctor or nurse.

79%	82%	81%	81%	80%	79%
Medica Value	Health-best	Wellness Plus	America Health	First Health	Prime Plan

Percent of members who said it was "easy" or "very easy" to get medical care when they need it.

80%	73%	74%	71%	70%	73%
Medica Value	Health-best	Wellness Plus	America Health	First Health	Prime Plan

Percent of members who said it was "easy" or "very easy" to get information from their plan about benefits and services.

60%	46%	52%	38%	46%	51%
Medica Value	Health-best	Wellness Plus	America Health	First Health	Prime Plan

Satisfaction: Detailed Member Ratings

The numbers in the boxes show the percent (%) of plan members who rated their health plan "very good" or "excellent."

HEALTH PLAN RATINGS:	Medica Value	Healthbest Northwest	Wellness Plus	America Health	First Health	Prime Plan
overall health plan	58	49	53	46	51	50
coverage for prevention	52	48	51	46	51	53
coverage for illness	55	51	56	49	56	54
choice of doctors	50	36	42	42	35	39

MY DOCTOR OR NURSE:	Medica Value	Healthbest Northwest	Wellness Plus	America Health	First Health	Prime Plan
shows personal interest in me	46	59	53	55	55	56
spends enough time on my visit	46	59	53	54	56	56
listens to what I say	61	67	63	63	66	65
explains things to me	62	72	67	66	66	69
gives complete exams	59	66	63	61	63	65
follows up on my case	50	60	51	57	57	58
tells me how to stay healthy	49	56	51	52	56	55
makes me feel better	51	58	51	54	53	56

Below Average ◯   Average ◍   Above Average ●

Source: 1996 Oregon Health Plan Consumer Satisfaction Survey.

Satisfaction: Detailed Member Ratings, Continued

The numbers in the boxes show the percent (%) of plan members who rated their health plan "easy" or "very easy."

HOW EASY IS IT TO GET:	Medica Value	Healthbest Northwest	Wellness Plus	America Health	First Health	Prime Plan
medical care when I need it	80	73	74	71	70	73
an appointment	65	76	70	70	62	69
needed medicines	83	82	79	81	83	79
emergency care	72	64	58	62	59	62
referral to specialist	52	49	49	47	48	51
medical advice (during hours)	71	62	59	61	59	58
medical advice (after hours)	52	39	37	37	41	31

HOW EASY IS:	Medica Value	Healthbest Northwest	Wellness Plus	America Health	First Health	Prime Plan
getting plan information	60	46	52	38	46	51
understanding plan information	61	50	57	46	51	54

Below Average ○   Average ◐   Above Average ●

Source: 1996 Oregon Health Plan Consumer Satisfaction Survey.

Quality: An Overview of Quality Measures

These scores show the percent (%) of plan members who received the care described within the specified time frame. *For example, 29 percent of the diabetic patients who are enrolled in Medica Value had an eye exam last year. For comparison, Oregon's Benchmarks (goals for immunizations and maternity care) are shown for the year 2000.*

	Medica Value	Healthbest Northwest	Wellness Plus	America Health	First Health	Prime Plan	Oregon Benchmark
Diabetic Eye Exam The percent of diabetic patients who had an eye exam last year.	29%	22%	32%	45%	42%	38%	*Not available*
Childhood Immunizations The percent of children who received all shots by their second birthday.	82%	55%	71%	63%	78%	78%	*100%*
Maternity Care The percent of pregnant women who saw a doctor or nurse in the first 12 weeks.	80%	89%	87%	88%	96%	91%	*95%*

Source: Estimates based on regional data.

A graph of each measure is shown on the next three pages.

Quality: Diabetic Eye Exam

One of the complications of diabetes is blindness. Loss of sight can be delayed with early detection and treatment. This graph shows the percent (%) of diabetic patients who had an eye exam during the last year.

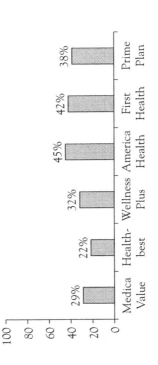

Oregon has no Benchmark for diabetic eye exams.

Quality: Childhood Immunization Rate

Getting children immunized (through shots) is one of the most important ways to keep children healthy. This graph shows the percent (%) of children in each plan who have received all the recommended shots to prevent certain diseases by their second birthday.

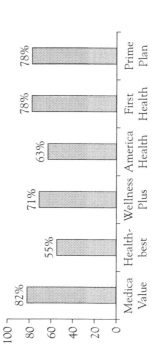

Oregon's Benchmark (goal) for the year **2000 is 100%.**

Quality: Maternity Care

Office visits to doctors or nurses early in pregnancy (maternity care) can help women have healthier babies. This graph shows the percent (%) of pregnant women who visited a doctor or nurse within the first twelve (12) weeks of their pregnancy.

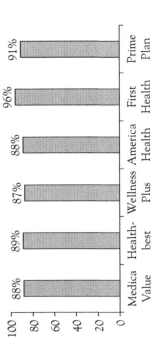

88%	89%	87%	88%	96%	91%
Medica Value	Health-best	Wellness Plus	America Health	First Health	Prime Health Plan

Oregon's Benchmark (goal) for the year **2000 is 95%.**

Worksheet: Choosing a Health Plan

➤ **Set your priorities.** Ask yourself, "What information is most important to me?" and then rank the topic/s.

➤ **Gather the information.**

Fast track—go directly to the pages that describe your # 1 topic; note the plans that meet your needs best. Continue through all topics that are important to you.

Easy does it—read about managed care, covered services, and plan differences, then go to your priority topics and "*fast track*."

➤ **Narrow the field.** List your top three choices.

➤ **Select a plan.**

Priorities	Topics	Health Plans I'm Interested In	Notes
◯	Doctors (page 5)		
◯	Hospitals (page 6)		
◯	Services (pages 7–8)		
◯	Satisfaction (pages 9–12)		
◯	Quality (pages 13–16)		
◯	Other		

My plan choice is _____ . Call 1 (800) 359–9517 to enroll.

Hotline: Consumer Scorecard Information

If you have questions or would like help using any part of this guide call the toll free number below to reach the Oregon Consumer Scorecard Hotline:

1 (800) 297-1234

YOU CAN GET ⟶ physician information.
⟶ help reading graphs and charts.

IF YOU WANT ⟶ information about a specific page, press the page number.
⟶ to speak to a real person, press "0."

You can access the recorded messages twenty-four hours a day; a real person is available from 7:00 a.m. until 10:00 p.m. Monday through Saturday.

Supplement: Special Topics for Mini-Guide

Often people have specific health concerns for themselves or a family member and would like additional information about the special services available to meet their individual needs. "Mini-guides" will describe the services available, the satisfaction of plan members who use those services and the quality measures for the health topic. Subject for the mini-guides are listed below:

- Depression
- Heart disease
- Asthma
- Breast cancer

- Diabetes
- Low back pain
- Arthritis
- Maternity care (pregnancy)

Sample mini-guide for maternity care is on the next three pages.

Mini-Guide: Maternity Care

A primary goal of the Oregon Health Plan is to provide a healthy start for mothers and newborns. Scheduling regular visits to a doctor during pregnancy (called prenatal or maternity care) is the best way to avoid difficulties during delivery and to have a healthy baby.

Sometimes events or circumstances in a woman's life put her and her baby at risk for problems during pregnancy. These include:

- Age (teenagers and women over 40 years old)
- Poor nutrition (especially lack of calcium, protein, iron, and folic acid)
- Health conditions (such as diabetes, anemia, or high blood pressure)
- Use of certain substances (alcohol, tobacco, and drugs)

For these women, prenatal care is even more important.

The Oregon Health Plan pays for prenatal care from the beginning of a pregnancy through delivery and follow-up for all eligible, enrolled pregnant women. The health plans in your area have developed policies and programs to ensure healthy mothers and babies. The comparison chart that follows provides answers to questions such as:

- What special maternity services do the plans provide?
- How satisfied were women with these services?
- How do these plans rate on quality measures?

Mini-Guide: Maternity Care Service Features

This table shows maternity service features available beyond basic benefits; the information was provided by the health plans in response to a 1996 survey.

	Medica Value	Healthbest Northwest	Wellness Plus	America Health	First Health	Prime Plan
Delivery Options						
Homestyle Birthing Rooms in all Hospitals	A	A		A	A	A
Option to Give Birth at Home		A				
Midwives Available	A	A		A	A	A
Education Services						
Birthing Classes	A	A	A		A	
Parenting Classes	A					A
Breastfeeding Specialists	A		A	A		
Patient Incentives						
Reward to Complete Prenatal Care			A			A
High-Risk Services						
Risk Assessment (ways to identify high-risk pregnancies)	A					A
Case Manager (person who organizes care in high-risk cases)	A				A	A

A = Service Available   Blank = Service Not Available

Mini-Guide: Maternity Care Satisfaction & Quality

	Medica Value	Healthbest Northwest	Wellness Plus	America Health	First Health	Prime Plan
Satisfaction Ratings[1]						
Overall Health Care Percent of pregnant women who rated the health care provided by their plan as "very good" or "excellent."	58%	59%	67%	57%	50%	53%
Overall Health Plan Percent of pregnant women who rated their health plan overall "very good" or "excellent."	63%	69%	67%	64%	45%	72%
Quality Measures [2]						
First Visit of Pregnancy Percent of pregnant women who visit a doctor or nurse within the first 12 weeks of pregnancy.	88%	89%	87%	88%	96%	91%
Care During Pregnancy Percent of pregnant women who had the recommended number of prenatal visits during the entire pregnancy.	54%	43%	50%	45%	60%	55%

[1] *Source:* 1996 Oregon Health Plan Consumer Satisfaction Survey.
[2] *Source:* Estimates based upon regional data.

A Request for Descriptive Navigational Information

The following descriptive information is being requested of all health plans participating in the Oregon Consumer Scorecard Consortium. None of the information requested exceeds that already required from OMAP as a term of participation in the OHP Medicaid program. We are requesting this information for the descriptive elements of the prototype scorecards that will be piloted tested during the month of April in select communities around the state.

The information requested flows from the OHPI staff memo titled "Oregon Consumer Scorecard Project: Components of the Prototype Scorecards" that was circulated at the February meeting of the Health Plan Committee (attached). This memo was reviewed by each of the Consortium subcommittees (Technical, Health Plan, and Consumer) at their February meetings, and all relevant changes suggested incorporated into this final draft.

Name of Health Plan _____

Name of Person Completing Survey _____

Phone Number of Person Completing Survey _____

I. Access Information: Primary, Specialist, and After-Hours Care

    1. Please provide a copy of your current PCP selection information (the list provided to new OHP enrollees).
    Questions:
      a. Do you routinely provide the physician/nurse practitioners board certification/s with new member information?
      Yes ❑   No ❑

b. Do you provide office location in the PCP selection information (e.g., address and/or city, township, etc. of physician's practice location)?
Yes ❏   No ❏

c. Do you provide public transportation information with the PCP selection information?
Yes ❏   No ❏

d. How often do you update whether a physician's practice is open to newly enrolled OHP members? _____

e. Do you provide this updated list to prospective or new members?
Yes ❏   No ❏

2. Please provide a copy of your current specialist panels information (the one provided to new OHP enrollees).
   Questions:

   a. Do you provide a listing of specialist panels to new members at enrollment?
   Yes ❏   No ❏

   b. If provided, do you list their board certifications?
   Yes ❏   No ❏

   c. If provided, do you indicate office location?
   Yes ❏   No ❏

   d. If provided, do you indicate office access to public transportation?
   Yes ❏   No ❏

   e. If provided, do you indicate at which hospitals specialists admit under the terms of your plan?
   Yes ❏   No ❏

3. Please answer the following questions regarding referral mechanisms to non-allopathic providers (e.g., chiropractors, naturopaths, acupuncturists, massage therapists).

   a. Does your plan *ever* authorize payment for the following practitioners for OHP members?

   Chiropractors   Yes ❏   No ❏
   Comment: _____

   Naturopaths   Yes ❏   No ❏
   Comment: _____

Acupuncturists   Yes ❏   No ❏
Comment: _____

Massage therapists   Yes ❏   No ❏
Comment: _____

   b. Please describe under what conditions, and by whom, authorization is made.

4. Please describe the protocols, guidelines, etc. *imposed by your plan* (i.e., not within the discretion of individual PCPs) for referrals to specialists by PCPs.
   Questions:
   a. Are referrals to specialists totally at the discretion of the PCP?
   Yes ❏   No ❏
   Comment: _____

   b. Are there any specific conditions where specialist referral protocols are specified by the plan (e.g., diabetics to endocrinologists)?
   Yes ❏   No ❏
   If *yes*, please specify conditions and protocols.

5. Please describe how **after-hours** advice and care is rendered to OHP enrollees in your plan. Be sure to specify triage procedures, including who members talk with when they call (e.g., answering service, nurse), and where after hours urgent care is provided (e.g., urgent care clinic, hospital emergency department, etc.).
   Attach description of 250 words or less.

6. Please describe how **emergencies** are authorized in your plan for OHP members. Be specific about the actual procedure a member must follow to assure that emergency room services are covered.
   Attach description of 250 words or less.

II. Coordination of Care (tracking referrals, care coordination, follow-up care)

1. Does your plan have an automated process whereby referrals between PCPs, specialists and/or non-allopathic providers are tracked to assure continuity of care?
   Yes ❏   No ❏
   If *yes*, please describe the process. Be sure to specify how individual patient records are *handled* once a referral is made.

2. Please describe how your plan assures that information about prescription drugs and DME is maintained in patient records for continuity of care purposes.

3. Please describe how your plan has implemented the Exceptional Needs Care Coordination (ENCC) function required by OMAP. Be specific about screening protocols, including who gets screened, e.g., some Phase II enrollees, all Phase II enrollees, all high cost enrollees (Phase I & II, etc.), who fills the role of ENCC (i.e., contract or plan staff, background and training of care coordinator), what services are actually provided, and level of coordination with outside plan services (e.g., agency case managers, social services, etc.).
   Attach description of 250 words or less.

III. Health Plan Quality Assurance Activities

1. Does your health plan have a consumer advisory committee/council comprised of OHP plan members?
   Yes ❏   No ❏
   If *yes*, please describe its composition, how often it meets, its functions.

2. Please describe your plan's QA Committee including who sits on it, how often it meets, and major activities.

3. Does your health plan undertake any condition-specific outcomes studies or other targeted quality improvement initiatives?
   Yes ❏   No ❏
   If *yes*, please describe the populations, conditions, etc. that are the subject of these studies and/or initiatives.

4. Does your plan provide financial incentives to PCPs (i.e., payment adjustments) for ANY of the following reasons?
   a. Consumer satisfaction surveys of physicians   Yes ❏   No ❏
   b. # of patient complaints or grievances   Yes ❏   No ❏
   c. Quality/outcomes measures   Yes ❏   No ❏

IV. Complaint & Grievance Procedures

1. Please describe the process established by your plan for handling complaints and grievances by OHP members. Be specific about the process

from simple to complex, beginning with an oral complaint through a formal adjudication process (who is involved, how many steps are involved, is there a plan-level ombudsperson, etc.).
Attach description of 250 words or less OR Standard Operating Procedures/ Protocols.

V. New Member Orientation & Education

1. Please describe how a new OHP enrollee is oriented to your health plan. Be specific about all mediums used including written materials, new member orientation meetings, telephone advice, videos, etc. Also, please indicate whether each new member is personally contacted about orientation activities, and at what point after the new member has enrolled that orientation begins.
Attach description of 250 words or less.

VI. Health Event Scenarios

1. For each of the following three populations, please describe in what ways, if any, your plan sets practice standards for its participating PCPs and specialists. Please be as specific as possible where protocols exist at the plan level and *attach any standard protocols your plan has developed.*

    a. **Maternity Care**   At what point is risk assessed? by whom? How is risk defined? Is a case manager assigned to a high risk mom? How is case management defined? How are social/environmental and behavioral risks handled? For a normal, low risk pregnancy, what choices exist for delivery (home style birthing, midwife services, etc.). Are enhanced services available to OHP women, e.g., birthing classes, lactation specialists, parenting classes?

    b. **Well Infant Care During the First Year**   Does the plan have practice guidelines about periodicity of visits during the first year of life? How does the plan monitor compliance with these guidelines? Does the plan offer CE or in-service opportunities for its pediatricians and pediatric nurse practitioners on content of care issues? Does the plan support a population-based immunization tracking system?

    c. **Management of Diabetes**   Does the plan have practice guidelines it encourages for the care of diabetic patients? Please describe. At what point in the treatment and follow-up care of diabetics are specialists used? Please be as specific as possible about the treatment protocols encouraged by your plan for the treatment of diabetics.

Please attach descriptions to individual questions as needed. Thank you for your assistance.

Name Index

Subject Index

A

Access, scorecard role in, 7

Accountability: alchemy of, 127–128; and quality, 116–117; and scorecards, 119–129

Agency for Health Care Policy and Research (AHCPR): and consumers, 42, 43, 47; funding from, 27–28, 98; and public policy, 6; and quality, 101, 102, 105

Aid to Dependent Children, 90

Aid to Families with Dependent Children, 29

American Association of Health Plans, 27, 84. *See also* Group Health Association of America

Associated Oregon Industries, 20

B

Benova, Inc., 28, 43, 44, 46, 59, 68

C

California Public Employees Retirement System, 42

Center for Health Policy Studies, 105, 114, 117

Center for Quality of Care Research and Education, 105

Children, as special population, 72, 73–74

Cleveland Health Quality Choice, 42

Client Satisfaction Survey, 60, 84

Clinical quality measures, relevance of, 14–15

Clinton administration, 1, 4

Competition, functions of, 4–5

Computer Model as Decision Aid, 28

Computerized Needs-Oriented Quality

Measurement Evaluation System (CONQUEST), 105

Consumer Assessment of Health Plans Survey, 6, 20, 42, 98, 105

Consumer health care scorecards. *See* Scorecards

Consumer Satisfaction Survey, 31, 79–80, 82, 83–97, 125

Consumers: and accountability, 122–123; attitudes of, 35–48; background on, 35–36; choice and voice of, 49–68, 127; choice issues for, 38–40; and clinical quality, 14–15; decision making by, 40; feedback from, 8, 57, 65–66; focus groups of, 43–45, 49–51; focus on individual, 26; information tailored to, 56, 66–67, 69–76, 123; information wanted by, 35–48, 52–57; interest levels of, 37–38, 105–107; knowledge base of, 36–37; and paternalism, 33; preferences of, 35–48, 128; quality defined by, 102–105; reporting to, 109–110; resources for, 20; rights of, 18; rural, 73–74, 90–93, 96, 121; satisfaction surveys of, 41–42, 44, 60–61, 77–99

Costs: level of sharing, 55; of scorecard production, 124–125

D

Data: collecting, 112–114; comparing, 108–109; denominator issues of, 110–111; secondary analysis of, 32–33

Decision making models, 40

Delmarva Foundation for Medical Care, 105

DEMPAQ study, 114

163

Printed and bound by CPI Group (UK) Ltd, Croydon, CR0 4YY

16/04/2025

14658444-0001